Crushed: When Parenting Is Hard

A Journey to Strength and Hope

Melissa Dayton

10% of the proceeds from the sale of this book goes to support the efforts of You Can NOT Be Replaced.

This book was written for the most broken of hearts. The one whose soul has been crushed by life but is strong enough to move forward, step by step, one day at a time.

"Your heart is greater than your wounds."—Henri JM Nouwen

TABLE OF CONTENTS

Introduction

Being a parent is an amazing gift. When our babies are first placed in our arms and we look into their eyes, our world changes. The experience can be one of the most profound and joyful in life. Caring for our children is a time of growth for us, as we let go of our own desires in favor of providing a life that will help them soar. But, life isn't that easy; what happens when parenting doesn't go as planned? Usually, by the time our kids are teenagers, we have realized parenting can be far more complicated than we originally thought. Sometimes, events leave us in a place that, emotionally, we didn't anticipate. We are left defeated, heartbroken, and crushed.

Parenting older kids can be an exciting time of growth. Watching a teenager perfecting the things they love, while having a ton of laughs, as they become a part of the larger community, is a real happiness. But, it can also be hard: frustrating, discouraging, and overwhelming. One of our favorite teachers says: "Small kids—small problems. Big kids—big problems." Whether our kids go through tough times because of mental health or addiction issues, phases caused by their own poor choices or the negative impact of others around them, circumstances of life can add burden and stress to the whole family.

Our job as parents is to help them navigate out of those situations and consequences while teaching a life lesson in the process. Occasionally, one of our children truly suffers during a time in their life, and we need to buckle down and lean in. That doesn't leave much time for ourselves or maybe even our other children. Those times can impact our other relationships in a negative way. Stressful situations in family life can lead to white-knuckle parenting, navigating in 'survival mode,' which creates a life of stress and can builds walls between those we love.

For us, the experience of being crushed came when our daughter, Emily, was a freshman in high school. In April of that year, one of the seniors at her school completed suicide. It was confusing, tragic, and something that we never expected our child would have to live through in our quaint beach community. Six weeks later, there was another boy. That fall, another. Sometimes, what happens in our child's life isn't the direct result of decisions that they've made, it's from a situation that surrounds them. That lack of control over what's happening can be defeating.

It's a tough culture to be a teen in, with high expectations for 'success' and no boundaries on life experiences they may not be mature enough to handle. Statistics are showing the effects on our kids with escalating suicide rates, opiate addiction, and binge drinking numbers. Every family has hard times, but when those times are overwhelming, they can impact us deeply. So, how do you use those tough times as relationship builders, not defeaters?

By the time Emily was a senior and graduated, our community had lost 6 boys to suicide. We were faced with a young lady who was shattered by what was happening within her peer group, though none of the losses were close friends. Each loss carved a deeper hole in her and made high school a painful experience. Emily graduated and went away to school, and we were hopeful for fresh beginnings. But, in February of her freshman year, we had to call to tell her that the school had lost another student to suicide.

She was completely heartbroken and crushed. This time, though, she got angry, and she looked at us and said, Don't they realize they can't be replaced?!" Emily wanted to order wristbands and for them to be passable from student to student. She wanted the students to have an excuse to approach someone they might not normally. We had no idea how that moment would redirect the direction of our lives. The wristbands passed from one student to another, local kids brought them back to their colleges, and began a grassroots movement. Four years later, over 50,000 wristbands have been passed all over the USA, Canada, UK, and Australia.

Our family ended up starting an organization based on social connection and building relationship through the passing of a simple wristband with words of kindness or gratitude. Social connections and bonds matter, and there was a need to cross social circles and strengthen those connections. We are looking to fill a communication hole and provide opportunities to get kids help. If we don't know they are hurting, we can't do that. Since we began, we have spoken to over 30,000 high school students, in addition to kids in our community and their parents. We didn't intend to start something, but we did.

During the cluster of tragedies at the high school, Chip and I stepped back from all our responsibilities. We left ministry, stopped volunteering, left book clubs and studies. If we had a dinner out, it was no longer on the weekend but a week night. We reached out to friends and mentors with older children and took the time to make sure we were providing Emily and her younger siblings a secure environment. Those intentional efforts protected our family and nurtured some strong bonds.

Chip and I are communicators; we are social and experienced parents. We have lived through three teenagers and have two at the moment. Some days, we feel we have done a great job, and sometimes, we feel like we have failed. That's parenting. But, as Chip says, there's not much you can say that would surprise or scare us.

Not only are we the parents of 8 children, but we have almost 20 years of youth and family program experience. The time we have worked with teens has made us better parents, and our time with other couples has given us a solid foundation in marriage. We have studied crisis and addiction, mental health, and the teen brain, but all that considered, the one thing we know to be true when impacting teens is simple: they want to know you care, you hear them, and you believe in them.

Time has passed; Emily graduated from college and is working a job she loves. Through her experiences, she says she established an incredible bond with not just Chip and myself but also her siblings. Her understanding of the grounding family can provide is the great gift that came from the sadness. She also learned the value of surrounding herself with good people, good friends, and others who helped her be her best version of herself.

Sometimes, life is very, very hard. Sometimes, experiences leave us crushed. While we really do not have control over some situations, we do have control over how we respond, and we can have profound influence. Crises and difficulties, when we work through them with help, can lead to great personal growth. That's hard to hear in the midst of struggles, but I promise there is light at the end of the tunnel, if you're willing to do the work.

As parents, when we intentionally shore up the structure that we have around our kids and focus on connecting with them, we become a safe place for them to work through hard times. Signs of stress are markers for times of growth. We need to take time to notice those opportunities in the mess. Please don't assume that all the answers are in this book, it is not intended to take the place of a counselor for your family or treatment for addiction. But you can use it in addition to those resources, and it will ease some of the stress. It would be unfair to say that parents who have been through heart breaking times simply didn't apply the things I talk about here. We know too many who did.

There's a tendency to read something and think, 'my sister should read this, my neighbor, my spouse.' Read it for you, as a parent, no one else. "Crushed" is intended to help you find your center again, so that you can do your best to reground your family. That starts with you. Your healing, the wisdom you'll gain, and your relationship with your child. If you're willing to do the work, you'll begin to breathe easier as you truly become a trusted person for your kids to turn to when they need a soft place to land.

YCNBR — The Beginning

"The human capacity for burden is like bamboo—far more flexible than you'd ever believe at first glance."—Jodi Picoult

On April 26th, 2008, my husband and I were out for dinner with friends. Our daughter, Emily, was a freshman in high school at the time and was home, taking care of our younger children. We got a text message from Emily in the middle of dinner, telling us that one of the seniors at the high school had taken his life. She was confused; she really wasn't even sure who he was, but she knew his name was Tim. Little did we know that that evening was going to change our lives forever. In the aftermath of losing Tim, the kids in the community were deeply grieving, and parents were confused and waiting for answers. Unfortunately, 6 weeks later, the community lost another young person to suicide; he was one of Tim's friends. That fall, there was another. Needless to say, everyone was numb. Our daughter, Emily, was profoundly impacted by each loss, but her questions always came back to Tim.

By the time Emily graduated from high school, our community has lost a total of 6 boys to suicide. When it was time to go to college, all of us were happy that Emily was going to have a fresh start. But, in February 2012 of her freshman year, the community lost one more boy to suicide; he was the last of the suicide contagion, bringing the total to 7. We had to call Emily at school and tell her, and then Chip went to get her and bring her home for the weekend.

Emily was deeply wounded; we talked for several hours at our kitchen table, going over the same old list of questions, and finally, she got angry. She looked at Chip and I and said, in frustration, "Don't they realize they can't be replaced?!"

As soon as the words were out of her mouth, all three of us knew there was something there. The core of the complexity of what was happening was explained in one simple question. The kids in the community needed to be reminded of their value. Emily asked, "Can we buy some wristbands? I want them to say 'I cannot be replaced.' We will have the kids wear them as long as they feel like they need them." Then, she looked at me, and she said, "but I think," (we said in unison) "they should be passable." She said, "Exactly. I want them to have an excuse or a prop that they can use to walk up to another student to cross a boundary they might not, normally, and say something kind, or maybe even thank them for being their friend."

We ordered 500 wristbands that said 'I can NOT be replaced,' and on the back, they say, 'Pass it!' We gave out the wristbands to the students, some mothers and fathers, and they were gone in two weeks. After we ran out, I was driving to class with a friend who was getting weekly updates on how quickly everything was coming together, and while we were talking, she texted a friend and asked if she would donate so we could buy another 500 wristbands. She did, and we passed another 500 out; they, too, were gone in a couple of weeks.

Many of the students who were in high school while Emily was there, brought wristbands back to college and began passing them to students on campus. A grass movement was born as they spread very quickly all over the country. We started receiving emails and Facebook comments from people of how they were profoundly impacted by someone approaching them. Now, just over four years later, there are well over fifty-thousand 'I cannot be replaced' wristbands being passed across the United States, Canada, UK, and Australia.

The power doesn't come from the wristband, though; it comes from the passion, courage, and, especially, kindness that people express when they reach out to another person. Social connection is powerful. Deeply ingrained in each one of us is a desire to be noticed, valued, heard, and loved. What we discovered was, sometimes, the answer to something complex is simplicity.

Over time, Emily was able to meet Tim's mom and ask all the questions she needed to. That meeting helped Em heal and understand. His mother, Lisa, is very open with her story and her grief. She has been an amazing resource and support for many grieving families and has written that story to help others. Her book is called *Without Tim*, and Emily, who is an artist, was able to work with Lisa and help to design the cover of the book. Lisa was and is a strong connection for Emily in her healing and hope, moving forward. The experience of the losses in our community changed Emily forever, but she has learned that, out of even the darkest times, good grows.

About six months after we started the organization, Hurricane Sandy hit our community, and we immediately started helping with recovery, coordinating volunteers, and helping connect people with resources. It was exhausting work, considering 1800 homes in our community were touched by wave and water damage. There was a great need to make sure that everyone is taken care of emotionally since now, the community was considered a double trauma area. We made sure that we brought in counselors to our distribution center, and even had events where counselors would come and meet the people in the community. With several other groups, we helped to sponsor a very large event focused on emotional healing in the aftermath. The hurricane added even another layer of stress and pain to what was, already, a rough couple years.

In the middle of the relief work, Chip and I received an email from a mom who had lost her son to suicide in 2010. She had found us through our friend, Lisa, who had just finished her book. This mom had noticed us listed on Lisa's website as a resource. She found that our positive message of hope and focus on kindness was exactly what she was looking for. We went to speak at her son's former high school during his celebration of life and from there, several others', as well. Since then, we have spoken to over 30,000 high school students, as well as parents and faculty.

What we do is slightly different from other organizations. As the wristband project grew, we began to be invited to county and state prevention group meetings. Because we came in late to the game, we knew there was no need for us to even try and reinvent what people were already working on, so we sat and listened carefully. We took notes from the perspective of community members and, especially, parents.

What we found was a lot of work was being done on studying trends and statistics. Most organizations were focused on crisis and the aftermath of a loss in a community, and keeping the funding to do so. Because there are many factors and complexities when someone has lost their battle with depression and taken their life, it was clear it was impossible for one organization to focus on all of the contributing influences.

We noticed there was a need to bridge valuable information between the people in communities and the 'experts'. There was not much work being done to try and reach kids several years before they ended up in crisis. Someone had to start focusing on the factors that could escalate a crisis that we may have more control over; ie: people, places and things, while teaching resiliency and coping skills. Finally, there was not enough boots-on-the-ground work being done with the teens so there was a huge disconnect to the reality of the culture they are living in.

The result of all of that listening was our focus. Our message is about of the value of life and strongly focused on relationships. Because, whether a student is living with clinical depression or not, how they take care of themselves, what they put into their bodies, and who they spend their time with is very important. We wanted to get very specific and focus on communication to improve their support systems. We knew that there were many teenagers who were trying to resolve problems on their own and were hesitant or even afraid to approach adults, and we knew we needed to try and remedy that.

Much of what we talk about is communication-based: ways to resolve conflict, understanding the importance of family, both the good and the bad. Equally important is surrounding themselves with good friends so that if they ever do end up in trouble or in a crisis, they will have in place the strong support to help them get to the right adult and work through the consequences.

Our program is meant to inspire teens to understand how incredibly valuable they are in the lives of others. Not just in their family, but also how immensely powerful they are in influencing one another. If they intentionally choose to impact others for good, to be brave, have courage, and use kindness, they could save a life. What we discovered, as we presented these things to the kids, was that they were profoundly moved.

We didn't intend to start anything; we just wanted to help the kids in our community here. The wristbands gave us the opportunity to take control and approach people we wouldn't possibly, otherwise. Did we end the cluster? No, we did not. Did we help improve the climate in the community? I hope so. Have the wristbands and our talks changed lives? Absolutely, and more so than we ever could have possibly dreamed. Counselors have told us there are people alive because of the work we have done. Kids have come forward and told us the same. This work we do is profoundly deep and close to our hearts. It is a passion and a calling of ours to remind young people of their irreplaceable value.

It has not been an easy undertaking, there are politics in nonprofit work that have caused us to walk away from a lot of the broader prevention work and simply focus on reaching as many young people as we can through speaking. There has been a layer of stress in our family with the added responsibilities, but our entire family, all of our children understand that, at the root of what we do is a deep, burning desire to make sure that what happened in our community does not happen again.

What we lived through with our kids was very hard. But, looking back, the lessons we learned have given us stronger parenting skills, an awareness of the culture our kids are living in, and deeper bonds with our kids. Crisis is temporary, though some situations last for a very long time. I hope sharing with you how we handled these situations may have a significant impact in helping you move forward.

A Rising Tide Raises All Boats

There is a level of denial when a community is in crisis because facing it head on is painful. There is a 'not in my backyard' attitude, it 'wouldn't happen to my kid', 'something must have been wrong there', because it is easier to encapsulate an issue than admit it is real. Those perceptions make it difficult to do prevention work. We need to stop labeling families who have children that are suffering as 'broken' and open our eyes to the reality that all families, regardless of their dynamic, are not immune to what's happening with raising mental health and addiction concerns.

If we shift to notice the lives of teens and young adults in our culture and admit that the growing numbers of addiction and mental health diagnosis have no socioeconomic boundaries, then we are more effective as a community of adults. If we can look up from the statistics, remove ego's and remember these are people's children, maybe more impact could be made. A strong community of adults creates an environment like a safety net where we can get the kids who are at risk help sooner.

We have more control over the contributing factors that could escalate a young person to crisis when we work together. No one group can eradicate what's happening; parents and communities need to be unified, which is easier said than done. It's hard for feelings and egos to be put aside and have an honest look at the mountain in front of our young people. But if we're going to reverse the climb of those numbers, we have to.

As adults, we need to do a better job instilling in them the knowledge that they are irreplaceable. We have a culture of young people who are equating their value in life to their accomplishments and what they produce. What happens to our kids when the 'plan' doesn't work out, and their identity that was wrapped up in all those accomplishments? If they have no other identity, they can feel like failures. Add in a mental health diagnosis or addiction issue and we start to understand 18–24 year olds being the highest risk age group for suicide. The pressures adults place on teens adds another layers of complexity. We have been left with a generation of young people who desperately need the adults in their lives to remind them of their value.

The cluster's impact on all the kids in our community will be life-long. It was a very real lesson on the fragility of life. I'm not sure, as a community of adults, we helped the kids grieve to the best of our abilities. The fear the adults experienced shut down many opportunities to let the kids grieve, heal emotionally and move forward. Some of the young people in the area have wrestled with serious addictions since; we've even lost some young adults to overdose. Some people say there isn't a connection, but I don't think anyone can say that with confidence. Too many kids who are now out of college have still recall their frustration to us. If grief is not allowed to progress, even in a healthy way, that grief becomes unbearable, and the kids begin to stuff their emotions and numb the pain. Some of the kids from the area don't want to talk about it; some feel like they were never able to.

We Are Socially Wired

From infancy we crave and survive from our social connections. Not only our physical needs are met, but our emotional sense of self and securities are grown socially through family and the other people who help to shape us. We need others in our lives. No one is meant to live this life alone, and no one is meant to carry burdens alone, we must be intentional and reach out to others. People suffering from depression or from addiction and people who are in crisis tend to isolate and keep to themselves. When we cross those social boundaries to make a connection, we give hope. We can't tell what someone is holding on the inside by simply looking at them. We need to be bold and break barriers.

What we learned from the experience of our community and the impact on our children is as parents, we aren't powerless. Parents are the primary educator and the ones with the most significant influence on our children. Even though they are 'big', they still need us and need to know that we are not going to leave them in their struggles. While you do not have control over all the decisions your child is making, what you do have is a profound impact over them. They want to be connected to you at the heart; there is no one they would rather see grateful, pleased, and happy with them than their parents. That never goes away, no matter how old you are.

My focus in writing this book is that yes, raising older kids is HARD, and this book, alone, won't resolve what needs medical attention. But, so often, after a talk, a parent will approach us and have questions, hoping we can send them in the right direction. I also receive calls from mostly moms, sometimes dads, who just don't know where to turn. Chip and I have our favorite resources we refer to, but we also have some tips from our experience that do help.

This book is similar to those conversations. The grounding of your family begins with you. Your healing, reflection and commitment to showing your child you are not going anywhere is the anchor. No matter what your family is going through, the coping your model to your teen and how you connect with them through the hard times, will make the difference in now they live their lives.

Grief, no matter how it happened, rocks a family. You can live through crises and come out on the other side.

Remember, the message is in the mess. The lessons you learn transform to life skills and will become wisdom that you can share with others once you reach solid ground.

JOURNAL

When were we at our best, as a family?

What made our relationships better?

Where is a special place we connect for bonding?

Can you carve out time to recreate now?

Please visit www.crushedwhenparentingishard.com to receive free printable journal pages featuring the art of Emily Dayton.

Making Family

"There is no one that is impacted more by my experience, education, and life lessons than my children. It will be them that spread my heart for the rest of their lives. They are my legacy."—Melissa Dayton

As parents, for the first time in our lives, we understand what it means to sacrifice our own comforts and wants for another person. That tiny person controls our every waking moment, even if we have other responsibilities. Having babies and small children is an experience filled with great joys and delights, as they discover the world for the first time. We bond and begin to see a deeper meaning to our own journey. As they grow, the act of parenting transforms us so much that we can't imagine life before we had them. They are our purpose, our responsibility, and we would protect them at all costs. Our hearts have forever changed, as we become transformed by our children.

It's true that having children changes us, emotionally, but did you know that the experience is not just a spiritual or emotional change but also a physical one? There is evidence that each baby that a mother carries leaves DNA behind in the mother's womb, so whether the mother carried the baby to term or not, cells are left in the woman's system. When we say, 'we carry them in our hearts forever,' that's not too far from the truth. For men, 6 weeks before their partner delivers, their testosterone levels drop. They become more nurturing and patient. Those levels stay low until about 6 weeks after the baby is born. While those numbers do raise again, after the initial six weeks, they never completely return to the level that they originally were.

For those of us who have had a hard baby, a cryer, colic, or the toddler who runs, crazed, and hits or bites other kids, the sacrifice becomes a complete gift of ourselves to the point of exhaustion. There is a humility and patience learned with an awareness that we cannot do these things alone. Extended family and friends become lifelines. We give so much of ourselves to them that there are days we think there may not be any of 'us' left. No one really 'gets it' unless they have lived life with a hard 'little.'[i] For most people, those babies find their way and settle. For some people, they are left with a challenging family situation that adds consistent stress to life, so life is not what they expected. Those families need the others to be kind and patient. But, we should not have to live this life alone.

For Chip and I, parenting has been all of those things, although having 8 kids wasn't on our radar when we were first married. We were high school sweethearts and had our first baby in college, so we were really working against the tides for many years. We learned so much from older parents and teachers that took us under their wing. Young families often struggle to find their voice as a family; that was true for us, too. It's hard to decide what to bring from our childhood and what we will create 'new' for our children. In addition to our parents, we had mentors, mostly older couples, that we spent time with. Some were from church, some were neighbors, and some were even our kids' teachers. They were great listeners, shared tips with us and helped us find that voice and confidence in raising our family our way.

While a big family was not clearly in my life plan, I do remember being about 11 and sitting on a big rock in the back of my childhood home's property by myself, thinking how much fun it would be to play in these woods with a whole bunch of brothers and sisters. In high school, I had friends with big families, who had great relationships with their siblings. There was some fighting but, almost always, laughing. As an adult, my friends, who grew up in large families, had bonds that ran very deep, and that intrigued me. I wanted my kids to have that kind of a family.

It took us a while to realize we 'own this package,' and we could create the family we wanted. Other people's expectations or perceptions of how we were raising our family were simply their opinions. Our family shouldn't be dictated by what others expected us to be. As long as Chip and I were on the same page, that's all that mattered. But, that's not so easy to do for some people, and other people's opinions and perceptions can be harsh and painful.

"8 kids—you must be nuts," is what we hear from most people, but we love our family, as crazy as it may be. We laugh when everybody asks us if we have a television or if we have any twins. Chip, especially, chuckles when he hears, "Same wife?" We get these questions all of the time. When we were younger parents, I used to get annoyed. If you can decide that your family is perfect and beautiful with 1 or 2 kids, then why can't we decide that we want to have a larger family? I would usually say something snarky. But, I've mellowed. I know that most people don't understand, and that's ok. I now know that not all people have the same lives, spouse, or faith. I know that families need moms to work full-time, and infertility is rampant. I understand I am incredibly blessed to have what was my heart's desire for a family, and it doesn't matter to me that people say outrageous things to us. I just smile while the litany of questions run, and usually, by the end, I hear, 'Well, I would have had more, but . . . well, God bless you,' to which, I reply, 'He did.'

Here's the thing: your life is your own, and it happens once. How you live it and how you raise your children is your decision. The voices and chatter of other people, as painful as they may be, do not define who you are as a family. Their opinions are not truth. Their opinions are their perceptions filtered through their own experience.

It's not typical that a mother of one or two children has any idea what raising eight children is like. She may have an opinion, may assume, because she feels she could never manage that many, I couldn't possibly. But those are her perceptions, based on her life. For me, unless a mom has birthed a large family or had a very similar experience to what is happening in my house, the comments, opinions, and judgements roll down my back. If one of my trusted friends, one who truly knows me, has a suggestion or notices something in one of my kids, I pay attention, regardless of how many children she has. They are usually coming from a place of wisdom and a sincere desire to help.

When you are going through a hard time and faced with criticism or constructive comments, ask yourself, 'who is the messenger?' I wish I had spent more time reflecting on this when I was a younger mom. I was usually wrecked by the opinions of some people that were very open with disapproval. If you are receiving a lot of judgement, take the time to consult some 'wisdom people' and share what has been said to you. But, remember, a mother who has never suffered with an addicted child, or a child who has a mental health diagnosis does not know what struggles you have and how you make it through your days. One who has had the experience will be a great asset.

If you are having trouble with your child, and family and friends are eagerly sharing their opinions and judgements, their perception of what you are doing or not doing may not be accurate. They are using their own experience to weigh your issues and find fault because, honestly, difficult times make most people uncomfortable. In their discomfort, they want to see the situation change, they may say some things to you that are pretty callus. Most of the time, they don't mean it, difficult situations leave people speechless and often they end up saying stupid things.

If you have someone in your life that also went through some tough times with a child, and they share with you some wisdom from their experience, listen closely to their words. They may not have all the answers for you, but there might be something in their experience that could make yours better. You decide; it's your family.

But, Eight? You Must Be Crazy!

Usually, when someone says to me, "Are you crazy?", I proudly say, "NO! I have been tested!" For the LaSalle University program I was in, I had to go through a day-long psychological screening to be accepted. This, of course, was a huge joke with my teenage children because they weren't so sure their mother was going to pass. I passed, and the results were very interesting. I was very proud of myself and still continue to pat myself on the back that the test showed I had *excellent problem-solving skills*, but the one thing they pulled out that I needed to watch was a need for 'control'. Ha.

Any mother with more than one child knows that the way we hold down the fort is with some kind of control. But, the control they were speaking of was deeper than just being organized. 'Control,' as I've tried to pay attention to it, is a defense or wall of security that we put up so that our flaws and insecurities remain unseen by others, as well as ourselves. We all have some control issues, whether passive or overt, that show up in our parenting. Times of stress usually bring out our inability to 'control,' and old, bad habits rear their heads as we move into survival mode. Understanding the motivation we have in times of stress is a great turning point in personal growth, if we take the time to reflect on it.

Beauty of 8

Children are a great source of joy, sacrifice, and our purpose in life. I know, when you read that, your heart said, 'yes.' We are parents. One of the beautiful parts of having eight children is that our family is this microcosm of society. Chip and I have learned more about ourselves and life from having a large family with so many different temperaments and personalities than any other experience we have had. Our family has given us a window into understanding others which I don't believe we had before.

But, I know that some people get stuck on our 'eight kids,' so before I say more, let me share my perspective with you. Some people want to know how we can possibly take care of them and love them all. That's a whole book in itself. But, what I can tell you is that love multiplies—it never divides. Each child welcomed into our home has brought incredible joy for all the people in the house; their distinct place and personality is a benefit to everyone. Whether two siblings are best friends and spend all their time together or they find that they butt heads often, they are forced to learn forgiveness and conflict resolution, and the experience is good. The family experience shapes us. We had dad of nine say to us once, 'You'll never regret the ones you have, but you may regret the ones you don't have.' For us, that is true.

We see siblings as a gift. Our kids have learned from the experience of brothers and sisters that they can't always be first. The smaller and younger kids need more time and have less patience while the older kids have more responsibility, but they have more freedom. They learn life is about all of us together, as a family, and not just the individual. So, the choices and consequences of decisions impact the whole family. That said, we have far more joyful times of celebration in a child's accomplishments and achievements, as well as birthdays, than we do negative times. There is a reality of human nature found in understanding that wants and needs are very different and that we have a great responsibility to share our gifts with others.

I love watching the older kids help the younger kids. For the younger kids, they look up to the older siblings and build bonds through those moments. The older kids also learn something about the value of taking care of those who need help. They have times they don't get along, but they usually work it out. Sometimes, we help but they need to resolve their own issues. Conflict resolution done well is a life skill that will help them all through their lives. Don't be afraid of that conflict in your family, but don't ignore it either. Some personalities are like oil and water, but they'll be siblings for life and they need to find a neutral spot for them to communicate.

Sure, there's an opportunity to be very, very busy and neglect one here and there, especially when one child is requiring a lot of attention. But, Chip and I have always been very conscious of that and keep each other in check. It is a tremendous amount of work, but it's not eight times the work. Honestly, as parents, you only take the bread and the peanut butter and jelly out once. You may only make two sandwiches while I make eight, but it still only happens one time.

The ups and the downs have molded us, and we've worked really hard to get to where we are. That doesn't mean it has been a cakewalk. Chip and I have been through some pretty horrible stuff; so much so, we used to say, when doctors would tell us odds and not to worry, our response would be, 'If something outrageous is going to happen, it will happen to us.' We have lived through the illness and death of a parent, children with medical issues, strange and bizarre, never-seen medical birthmarks, and illnesses that ended us up in specialty hospitals, multiple times with multiple kids. We've gone through issues with each other that almost ended our marriage twice, and we've lived through five teenagers.

Journey of the Teen Years

Having teenagers is fun, great big laughs, most of the time. But, they take way more attention than you may think than when they are little. There is a very real argument that they need you as much now as when they were babies. Being in a solid place, emotionally, to get through those years is important. It's when you see the best and the worst of what they learned. It's also when you see the bad patterns forming that you missed, now becoming harder to squash.

The awareness that people repeat patterns from their childhood should bring us all to our feet, as parents. All of us bring baggage from family history: old patterns and bad habits that become filters of how we perceive events. Families also pass along addiction and mental illness that pepper how we may see the world. We need to be aware of family history and those diagnoses. It takes intentional work to only bring the good we learned from our core family into our parenting and replace the bad patterns with something healthy. It's much easier to ignore the hard stuff and simply live each day, going through the motions on the surface. But, living that way is how those things creep through, unnoticed.

One of the concerns with raising teenagers is that we aren't the only ones influencing them. They have independence, for the first time, and are meeting tons of new people. There could be other people, outside our control, who are involved in our kid's lives. Hopefully, those are good influences, like coaches and teachers who help them discover their gifts in life. Those relationships can be lifesavers, or they can be contradictions and add a lot of stress.

We need to be the ones who, 'love them more,' as one of my mentors says. We, as parents, owe our children our time. It's such a short span of high school and college before they leave us, and their formation is our responsibility. There is nothing worse than a kid who goes looking for 'family' elsewhere. Once they bond, it's hard to bring them back, and if the bond is with a negative influence, the door could be opened to pain. We need to intentionally carve out time to be the trusted adult in our children's lives. They need us to.

For our family, time together is our lifeline. No matter how far they go into the world, they will always need a landing place to regroup and rest. We make it a point to instill memories and times that are good to help when things get hard. Deep roots always bring them back, and it's fun for the little kids to hear stories of when the big kids were their age. Simplifying to intentionally create those times together in your calendar helps to shape memories that could be a saving grace for your family too.

Making Family

The evolution of the timeline of life that happens when we spend time together is how families find their shape and character. We use babies as our timeline when telling stories in our house. Usually, something along the line of, "Well, who was I pregnant with? Who was I nursing?" It's similar to the Irish using pubs as mile markers; pregnancy and nursing is how we figure out the time frame of events in our life. Funny as that is, that evolution of creating a large family is our story. It is part of our 'making family.'

Chip and I were out for dinner one night in the midst of the cluster. I was overwhelmed and wishing we could go back in time to when things were easier. Our conversation went deeper into *why* life was easier, what was it about that phase of life made us feel like life was more stable and fulfilling? Obviously the fear of what was happening was vast, but we couldn't help but wonder if could identify some key simple factors of that time in life, maybe we could intentionally try to implement them into our daily life again and bring some peace back. The time we pin pointed was right before our oldest went to college.

It was when our fifth child, Meg, was a baby, life was good. Our days were peaceful, and everyone was happy. We had good people around us and were spending a lot of time with other big families, whose children were the same ages. The kids had good friends in those families. Everyone got along, and no one was ever left out. The guys would meet for book club, and the girls would meet during the week for different things. It was a time, not just of peace, but also growth. Those families made us better.

Good friendships can be a lifeline for times in life that are rough, but they also share in our joys and memories as well. I spent a lot of time, while I was pregnant with Meg, with a younger friend named Cathy. Cathy is a spark and so much fun to spend time with. Our conversations were not only deep and faith-filled but also trivial and ridiculous. She would pray for the most broken of society, as well as the 'perfect bikini' for summer, and discuss it all in the same conversation. We were both expecting babies right about the same time and had baby boy toddlers the same age.

Cathy was only in our area for a very short time. She and her husband moved out to San Diego right before the birth of both our babies. Before she left, she gave our family an incredible gift, even though it seemed trivial at the time. As we expanded the family with the fifth baby, we were also expanding the house. We were adding a big eat-in family room off the back, and I needed some kind of table to accommodate my large family for meals.

One day, she called me and said, "I stopped in town at the antique shop, and I found the table for your new room!" I said, "You found me a table?" (I wanted to pick out my table). She said, "It's fantastic! It's a big, long, farm table. I think it is at least 8 feet long, and it's BLUE." I said, "Oh, Cath, I don't want a blue table." She said, "No, no, no! This table's fantastic. It's going to fit right in the back of the new room; it's going to be the place where your family creates memories: where you'll have dinner every night, tell stories, and play games. It's just going to be perfect!" We bought that table, and to be honest with you, EVERYTHING happens at the big blue farm table. She was right.

The blue table is where we eat, the kids do homework, play games, paint, and create. It's where we laugh, discuss, cry, and it's where we created You Can NOT Be Replaced. The blue table is where Chip and I work every day and where we've written our talks. It's where I'm writing this book. The big blue farm table is the grounding center of our family.

We can't repeat those times, they are now just sweet memories. But what we could bring back was the focus on family time together and making sure we had times with the kids that were light, fun and a break from the seriousness of the current day to day. There was also a reminder to Chip and I that we needed to have good people around us.

The time in our life when we bought this table was an incredible gift because those relationships helped us form our family. Those families helped us create the family WE wanted. But, life changes, and that time drifted away. The older kids grew up and went to college, some of the families moved, some of the women went back to work, and the men's group dissolved. We all moved on into our own business with the kid's schedules and lives. We still occasionally see one another. It's not the same, though, and we do miss them.

Things Change

We had no idea life would get difficult for us like it did. We have since been through some very hard times as a family. Not only did we live through a 4 year suicide cluster, but also, a major hurricane hit our community in 2013. For 4 months, 7 days a week, we ran a distribution center, organized volunteers, worked with other town groups, and connected families to resources. We also dispensed over $100,000.00 in relief money. Those months were taxing on our marriage and our kids. It was almost inhumane what the families went through and how difficult it was to find them resources. We also lost our sustainable income when the government closed the golf course Chip ran.

Our three oldest kids went off to college and moved on. Two are done, and the oldest is in seminary. Life is very different. As the kids get older, it's becoming a rare thing to have a full table. I often stand as I'm putting the food on the plates, watching the kids as they all gather and take their places. They argue who's going to sit over next to Dad and how the supposedly 'favorite child' always gets the spot that they want. I love how one sibling sits very close to his sister so that his elbow is almost in her lap. When they were toddlers, that's how they always used to sit together, connected at the hip. It's a great joy to stand and to look at this incredible family that we have. We've worked hard: really, very hard, to create this life to give them a foundation and a center. The table is the symbol of that in our home.

I cherish the memories of the intimacy and of 'making family' that we've given the children. It's not the table; it's the relationships and the life that's built around it. Time with my kids is one of my cherished joys in life because I was able to have the family I wished I had grown up in. The gift of that blue table is with us every day; it's a joy marker for me, reminding me of a simpler time and giving me hope that, one day, we'll have times like that again.

As idealistic as our family may seem sometimes from the outside, we've been through some pretty unimaginable experiences. I had someone mock me once responding to me saying, 'How Norman Rockwell of you'. Those snarky remarks sting, life is not perfect for anyone, and we've had tough times. Some of those times have been deeply wounding and left us wondering if we were going to make it through; others were just another layer to what was already difficult. But we dug down, pulled together and came out on the other side, stronger and wiser. The gratefulness for our family comes from that hard work.

Dealing with Stress and Finding Center

If you're going through a difficult time with your kids, please remember—life happens in the mess: the good, the bad, the sad. Conflict and stress can be chaotic, and we need to choose to come back to center. My center is around that table. During the worst of what we went through, we still had our time together there. As parents, if we don't intentionally choose to focus on what matters, our relationships can be hurt, instead of built up. I really do believe that, while we make memories in the happy times, we build deep bonds working through hard times. But, we have to face them.

We need to strip away all the external business in life and really look at the heart of what's happening in the family. Open up, be honest, and face what's in front of us. If you're in the middle of a mess, stop beating yourselves up, every family has issues. Every family has bad patterns that they need to try and replace with better skills. I know there is more to what many of you are going through than can be solved with a nightly dinner at the table. I wish I could tell you it was that easy and a meal is all you have to do to bring peace back to your home. There are usually many contributing factors to situations, so patience has to be exercised as well as you can while you work through hard times.

Imagine the old, bad, relationship patterns are rocks. If you put those rocks into a basket and had to carry them around all day, it would start to get heavy at some point. Put down the basket. Take each rock out and look at it; how did it get there? Work through old patterns, heal the wounds, and find a better way to interact with others. When you do, you release the burden and give yourself a gift. Grounding yourself with stronger coping skills will help you come back to center and parent from a place of strength. Then, what you pass along to your children are solid patterns and healthy relationships.

Start by finding your center as a family, a starting point to build bonds. In our house, it's the blue table. For you, it could be in the car driving your kids to school or sitting in the same spot on the beach on a Saturday afternoon. If you don't feel like you have a place right now that you connect, take the time to reflect on when life was easier. Where did you have times of connection? Was it in the backyard? Was it going for a walk with the dog? What was it? You might have to really dig and find that place, but that place is important. It is symbolic of what your family needs emotionally, an anchor.

The process of finding that place to reconnect with your child may require taking time for quiet reflection. Finding those answers are why simplifying and stopping unnecessary activities is important. The space you will create will help you integrate better patterns into family life. Find that point where you can sit together and reconnect. Create that space again or a new space to rebuild and strengthen your family. Increase the trust and move forward.

Wouldn't it be so easy if we could just fix situations quickly? We can't. Parenting is a marathon, made up of several different roads and paths: really, more of a triathlon. Frustratingly, sometimes, we haven't trained for portions of it because we never thought or expected we would have the issue looking us in the face. While you may not have complete control, you do have a profound influence over your children. You are the voice in their head and the captain of the ship. You control the tiller in the back of the boat, a tiller that moves a rudder UNDER the water.

Dig deep and parent from a place of strength. Impact your family in a positive way. Make sure that what you are teaching them comes from a grounded parent that sincerely wants to influence them. Take care of your own wounds and plant your feet on solid ground. You have the opportunity, every time you have one of these conflicts, to teach them a nugget of wisdom that will become a part of their pattern and create a stronger you.

- 'When were we at our best, as a family?'

- 'What made our relationships better?'

- 'Where is a special place we connect for bonding?'

- 'Can you carve out time to recreate now?'

JOURNAL

Who are the like-minded parents in my life?

What is my child's greatest character trait?

Who can I bring in to help develop that gift in my child?

Have I taken the time to cry and heal?

Please visit www.crushedwhenparentingishard.com to receive free printable journal pages featuring the art of Emily Dayton.

Flipped Upside Down

"In each family a story is playing itself out, and each family's story embodies its hope and despair."—Auguste Napier

The night Andrew had alcohol poisoning was life-changing. The night began with a strange peace. Our big kids were out and accounted for, and the little ones being put to bed. Our oldest was just graduated from college and living at home while working his new job. For some reason, he was home that night, thank God. While I was upstairs, putting the baby to bed, I heard Chip say, "G*& D*&^m kids!" Then, he slammed the front door. That, alone, was completely out of character. I'm the reactor; he never responds to anything like that. I quickly put the baby in her crib and came downstairs. Christopher looked like a deer in the headlights, and I asked him, 'What was that about?' He said "Emily called, crying; it sounds like Andrew's been drinking.' What? How much? She's crying? How bad is he?

I called Emily and could hardly understand her through the tears. "He's passed out! He's white and drooling! This guy at the party put him in my front seat and started banging on the roof of my car, shouting, "Get him out of here," so I just pulled up around Lake Como. (Lake Como was about 2 blocks from the pavilion on the boardwalk where the party was being held). Is Dad almost here?!"

Chip went to meet Emily where she was parked. Chip transferred Andrew to our car so he could bring him home. The adult who hosted the party should have called us, and then an ambulance. We understood he was probably mad and didn't understand how bad Andrew was, but he left a 17-year-old kid in charge. Thank God Emily called us right away. I hung up with Em once Chip got to her and quickly called a friend who was a nurse and had older kids. I told her what Em said and asked her how I would know if we needed to go to the hospital. She told me to check his vitals, etc. I went upstairs and changed back into my clothes, just in case, and called Chip.

On the other end of the phone was the same frantic tone but this time from my husband. "I'm almost home; I don't know. He's passed out; I can't talk. Hold him up and drive at the same time! I'm almost home!" He pulled into the driveway and opened the front passenger door. There was my strong, healthy son, passed out and white as a sheet in the front seat. There was no question or even stopping to do what my friend said; we were going to the hospital.

That was a mistake. We should have called an ambulance immediately, but we had no knowledge of alcohol poisoning. In our day, kids who drank too much usually had overdone it at a keg and went to the hospital to get their stomach pumped. But, what teens are now drinking is hard, flavored alcohol. They put it into plastic water bottles and end up drinking three times more than the limit for binge drinking in one night. To make things worse, they pregame with a Monster caffeine drink. The result is that 5,000 young people die each year in the USA from binge drinking.

We both tried to pick him up and bring him to the back seat; I dropped his feet, not realizing how heavy he was. Finally, Chip got him in the back. I ran to the other side to sit with him, and we left. He was drooling, cold, and spitting. A mile down the road, Chip curses again! 'G&dd&^m kids!' What now? 'The light is on!' No gas. A couple miles later, we were stuck behind a little old lady doing 20 miles an hour. Honestly, it seemed like a 15 minute ride was an hour.

I was mostly focused on Andrew. When he was three, he suffered from night terrors so much that he knew the Saint Michael prayer before his alphabet. So, I placed my hand on his head and said the prayer for him. I, then, noticed that he was not breathing regularly. I leaned over and shouted in his ear, knowing that hearing is one of the last things to go, 'Andrew Dayton, you are in the best shape of your life—you open your mouth and breathe!' He parted his lips and took a breath. Three more times, I repeated the command on that ride when I noticed him lagging, and three more times, he responded.

Sometime during that ride, Chip must have called the ER to tell them we were coming. As we pulled in, a big male nurse, whom we later found out was a hockey referee (thank God), came out to meet us. He opened the back door of the car and exclaimed, 'OH! 15 *years* old! NOT a 15 month old unresponsive!' He said 'What's his name?' He proceeded to mildly slap his face one, two, three times, saying his name. Nothing. He took his fist and gave him a sternum punch, 'Andrew!' His eyes flashed open and then closed. The nurse looked at me and said, 'That's good—he's not in a coma.' He, then, proceeded to pick up my son like an infant and raced him into the ER.

What followed was a violent arrival. Clothes were cut off, and Andrew having a flight-or-fight response. He was thrashing, spitting, and cursing. It was unlike anything I had ever seen. Four adults were needed to hold him down so they could put IV's in both arms. Finally, at the foot of his bed, I put on my biggest mom voice and demanded, 'ANDREW DAYTON, THAT'S ENOUGH.' He stopped, and his face scrunched up, as he cried 'I'm sorry, Mommy—I'm sorry.' Then, he passed out cold.

They had to catheterize him because he was so unresponsive that they weren't sure he was only intoxicated. I questioned them, in my ignorance, because, quite honestly, this kid wouldn't even drink soda during soccer season and, to our knowledge, had never been drunk before. I relented and then had to leave the room. I could hear his screams from across the ER floor, 'Mommy, Mommy!', as if he was four years old. It was heartbreaking, frightening, and deeply sad.

When I came back to the room, he was unconscious and still very cold; his body temperature was 95°. We didn't know it at the time, but the ER was considering moving him to Trauma for warm fluids. Thankfully, Andrew was very healthy, and his oxygen levels slowly returned, as his temperature rose. I asked them to bring warm blankets; you know, the kind they give you after you have birth. In my head, that would be enough, but the nurse gave me a snide look, like 'stupid parents' was going through her head and walked out of the room. There was a strange vibe from the staff, except for the hockey ref.

Andrew's best friend's dad, who had been with Chip by the lake, had followed us to the hospital. His son was with Andrew at the party, so he came to tell us everything he could about what they drank and how much, as we tried to piece the night together. In all of the mess, we were not oblivious to the kindness and love of our friend, following us up that night, and my friend who was the nurse. She was one of our close friends that we had spent so much time with when the kids were young. Her kids were close with our older children. I didn't know until weeks later that she had hung up with me and texted all of her five children to pray for Andrew, which they did.

About two hours in, a nervous resident doctor came in and told us they wanted to do a CT scan. Andrew was still so unresponsive that they thought perhaps, he had fallen and hit his head. I fought them. Now, I was in a little denial, but when I was in high school, my dad's company made the MRI. I was aware the CT wasn't the best for all circumstances, and I also knew about the kickbacks some hospitals got for using them. I was chastised, so I relented again. I watched them put my son into that CT scan on a sheet, limp and lifeless. That was the moment for me when I became scared for real. I thought, for sure, that moving him would wake him up.

Back in the room, I sat, looking at the cheesy art on the wall and wondered. This kid was so hard, so hard to take care of when he was little. I had put so much of myself into his discipline, character, and safety. I was so sure the depth of his thinking and giving spirit was going to move mountains someday, but was this the end? All that for what? It was a place I never dreamed I would be.

Sitting next to our son, we seemed to be in a scene from a movie. There is nothing like sitting next to your child in an emergency room, waiting and wondering if he will wake up. Every once in awhile, I would get up, go over to him, and say his name, touching his arm. Nothing. I always thought if I ever had a loved one in the hospital in a coma, they would, for sure, hear my voice and squeeze my hand. I was wrong. He wasn't in a coma, though he was close. Every once in awhile, one of the pissed-off female nurses or the resident would come in to feel his extremities, checking for hypothermia. They would take his temperature and check his pupils, which were small and fixed. They wouldn't look up; they said nothing and would walk out.

Hospitals are a strange timeless vortex with buzzing fluorescent lights where hours are spent waiting. That night, we sat and sat. I expect other parents who have had a child overdose or end up with alcohol poisoning know the deep pain of watching your child suffer from a choice they made that you had no control over. I'm pretty sure an ER staff sees so many horrible things that a dumb kid taking a life-threatening chance makes them mad. 'What a waste,' they must think. For a parent, though, regardless of how your child ended up in that hospital bed, no matter how old they are, they are still your child and are in a very scary situation.

Finally, after four hours, the resident came back in to tell us that she had to check for one more reflex: the gag reflex. She was very nervous, to the point of shaking and was afraid to come in because she thought she was going to have to tell us there was nothing else they could do for him. We paused for a moment.

I went over to the other side of him, worried he would kick and fight again but also worried that this night was getting worse. The resident talked to Andrew to tell him what she was going to do, although he was still out cold. I held his hand. She slowly put the popsicle stick in his mouth and before she reached the back of his throat, his eyes popped open. She jumped back and let out a deep breath. I said, 'Andrew! You're in the hospital—Dad's here, too. We're SO glad your eyes are open!' He focused his light blue eyes on me and then started to cry. 'SO STUPID,' he said, and I agreed.

The rest of the night was somewhat of a whirl of movement. They put him into the ICU overnight, and repeatedly, our male nurse said to us, 'You are so lucky; you almost lost him tonight.' Then, he would repeat it to Andrew. It took four full bags of fluids with IV's on full before Andrew woke up. We had a miracle. Chip spent the night with him, even though he asked for me. I ended up having to leave because of the baby, who was still nursing and would get up at night.

I walked out of that hospital at 3:30 am with a security guard, who walked me to my car. I got in, still in shock, turned on the car, and had no gas. I prayed for a gas station to be open and thankfully, found one. I got home, and the door was locked. My kids had locked me out. My dog, who usually barked at leaves when they hit the window, stood, looking at me with his bone in his mouth and wagging his tail. Finally, I walked through our gate to the back door. My 9 year-old heard the gate and woke up Christopher.

I opened my laptop and went to Facebook. I went to Andrew's page. All I saw in the posts were comments like, 'You're the MAN!', 'That was awesome!', and pictures: pictures of my intoxicated, hardly-able-to-stand young son. There was another young lady at the party, passed out on the bathroom floor, and her friends thought posting that picture would be funny. One-by-one, I private messaged all those kids and asked them to take down the pictures, telling them we had almost lost him. All the kids responded positively. We need to give kids credit when they do the right thing.

The next day, I had to bring him clothes and pick them up. Andrew was waiting for his mom; I just couldn't get there fast enough. It seemed to take forever. I walked through the corridors of the hospital, dazed and a little uncomfortable, to be honest. Then, it happened; I walked through the big atrium central area right through a group of VERY pregnant women on a tour. I got incredibly sad. It wasn't that long ago that was us, hugely pregnant with this baby, not knowing what they would be like or what lied ahead. They were preparing to bring their babies home for the first time, with great expectations. I was going up to get my baby for the start of his new life, his second chance: a chance he almost didn't get.

In the days following Andrew's night in the hospital, our family was in shock. Emily was shattered; again, she had saved her brother. However, she also had known what he was going to do, so she was guilty. She and Andrew were very close, and she was not prepared for him being angry at her. It was weeks and then months of them working through that, and sadly, I'm not sure they have 100% returned to the closeness they had before.

Our response, like I had said in the beginning, was to use his fresh start as a teaching opportunity. We decided not to scream, not to shame, but to make the aftermath memorable. We wrote a note to Andrew's friends because we knew we had a 24–48 hour gossip window and had him send it to 15 people that he thought should know what happened. Of course, the kids passed it along to many more, which is what we wanted.

The response from the note was good. The kids knew how easily it happens, and they got it. The next week at school, only one kid made a snide remark to him, but the other kids stood up for Andrew. Sadly, the story faded and was forgotten when, a couple weeks later, another young girl did almost exactly the same thing. We understand Andrew chose to drink and showed up at that party drunk. He wasn't served there. But, the adults that night failed, including us. He needed the ER, ASAP, and we all acted later than we should have.

Binge Drinking

Binge drinking is defined by how many drinks a person consumes within an hour. This typically happens when men consume 5 or more drinks, and when women consume 4 or more drinks, in about 2 hours.[ii] Binge drinking leads to alcohol poisoning. When someone has alcohol poisoning, they need IV therapy to save their life. The hospital staff saved Andrew. We even brought him back a week later to thank them, to meet the people that made the choices that led to him coming home. We also wanted them to see what a great kid he was. They told us that no one had ever come back, and they were thrilled to have the opportunity to talk to him!

Had his friends brought him home and placed him on his side so he didn't choke on vomit and didn't get in trouble, we would have lost him. Had we gotten to the hospital an hour later, we would have lost him. Kids need to know that, in many States now, there is legislation that gives them immunity when they call to rescue a friend who has alcohol poisoning or a drug overdose. They have to be taught to do the right thing.

Teens don't measure when they're sneaking alcohol, drinking straight from the bottle. Based on his official blood alcohol level, which was .278, two hours after he was found on the boardwalk, and considering that number drops every half hour, there's a chance he was up around .310 at peak. I did some calculations, based on Andrew's body weight and the time, I came to 12–15 shots. I even got a bottle out and poured 12 shots out of it and asked him, a week later, if that's about how much. He said 'More.' It was dumb, impulsive, and illegal, and as Andrew said, 'Stupid.' But, good kids, very good kids, make very dumb choices that, unfortunately, can be life threatening. Those choices are often out of our control and leave us in a place we didn't expect.

There are a couple things that are important to how we handled the situation: Thankfully, I had had a conversation with my close friend, months earlier when she had shared a similar experience with her daughter. Her openness and honesty allowed me to see that these things do happen, and there's no shame in it. The cluster already had Chip and I very tuned into the importance of listening and responding well to our kids. We were keenly aware of noticing emotions, even though we were still blindsided by this night. Lastly, that moment of walking though the group of new moms on tour of the hospital was a distinct gift to me. It forced me to pause and recognize, in the moment, the opportunity to start fresh. The aftermath and how we choose to work through it determines a lot for our relationship with our kids.

Some people may have thought the note we sent out on Facebook was over the top, but honestly, it was as much for the adults to read as the kids. Adults, too often, turn their heads from drinking, but they need to know how easily alcohol poisoning can happen. I wanted parents to know what to look for and what to do if they were in the same situation, and I also wanted parents to remember adults are supposed to be on the same team.

Parents need to pull together as a community. We learn from one another, and we need each other as we help our kids. No parent has the right to allow a child to do something illegal; no parent has the right to usurp another parent's authority. The answer isn't to allow the kids' risk-taking behavior, as long as you're there. The trend to allow the kids to drink while you take their car keys doesn't mean they are safer home with you. If you allow your kids to get drunk at home, there's an 80% chance they will drink outside the home.

Days after we were home from the hospital, there was an article in a woman's magazine about a young girl who died in the basement of a friend's home with the parents present after taking 15 shots. We have heard stories of kids trying heroin for the first time in a basement, fully furnished with all the amenities the kids could want and parents upstairs. Kids have told us stories of what happens while parents are home that would make your hair stand on end. We don't have the right to make decisions like that for someone else's kids. What we do have the responsibility to do is share what we've learned, follow one another to the hospital, and support one another when we struggle.

If you don't have adults around you that are like minded, I ask you to reflect on where you can start to look to build some good relationships. It's the essence of true community. From families to towns to larger culture, we are all interconnected. There is not one thing that happens to us that doesn't impact the people connected to us, either positive or negative. When one suffers, like during the suicide cluster, we all suffer. When one is thriving, if done with humility, others can follow.

What Did We Learn

After a lot of reflection, I noticed I had missed some things. While I knew that my son, who had played varsity soccer since freshman year, seemed to have lost his confidence on the field, I didn't make the connection to that being a real self-esteem issue. He was a sophomore and feeling the pressure of having 'the only parents who don't allow drinking,' as well as academic stress. Boys are tough, and some don't open up. I would ask if he was ok, and he would immediately shut me down, "I'm fine. I know what you're going to say, Mom. I'm fine."

What I didn't know was he had a teacher that, for the second year in a row, was playing mind games with him. She was emotionally unpredictable with expectations that kept changing. He must have reminded her of someone because, as I found out, she was harder on him than any of the other kids. He didn't tell me this was happening, and slowly, his self-esteem declined. Combine all those things, add a break up with a girl, and a couple months later, you have a bad, impulsive decision, attempting to make himself feel good.

On the plus side of that, seeing how profoundly he wanted to be 'liked' by the unlikable, I knew I had an opportunity to take his need for security and validation from others and use it to his benefit. He needed people other than us to help build him up. The summer came quickly, and I decided to use math as an excuse to do some esteem boosting. I did some digging by going to my kids' favorite teacher and told her what I was hoping to accomplish. She recommended a teacher at the high school that was strong in character and understood my desire to rebuild Andrew's self-esteem from a good place.

The teacher did just that. I had mentioned that I wanted to focus on Andrew's strengths: compassion, giving, and doing for others. I told him one of his favorite things to do was go visit our good friend's autistic son. Andrew has a soft spot for kids in the autistic spectrum and is gifted with students that are special needs. He had a heart of gold, and it needed to be nurtured and recognized. The tutor shared books with him, got to know him, and even went so far as to arrange work with some special education students across the street at the elementary school. He was a teacher that understood giving to others was a huge esteem builder and that using gifts to do so was the channel. It worked. My son healed, grew strong, and never looked back.

Asking my teacher friend for a recommendation was one of the smartest moves I made. You can find those strong people; you just have to be willing to open up and ask. Remember, you aren't alone and aren't supposed to work through these things by yourself. You may have to gather courage and ask for it. Recently, my Matthew said to me, "But, Mom, I'm not brave; I'm scared." To which, I told him, "That's what being brave is: doing something with all the courage you have when you ARE scared." You have to find a way to still navigate from a place of strength while being gentle and forgiving with yourself.

We learned so much from the recovery of that night: about our family, how strong we really are, and the opportunity to learn and share that information to benefit others. I know you many have a long, ongoing situation, but the same pattern of healing is possible if you make the effort to surround yourself and your child with good people. Honestly, that night and its story has saved lives and hopefully, will continue to do so. We are very lucky.

They Can't Be Defined by Their Mistakes

I'm very aware that our one night doesn't compare to the depths of emotional wounds some of you may have experienced. Your situation could be very different from a teen's mistake. It could be an illness, financial issues, developmental delays, or loss of a family member. If you or your child has been through something tragic where others were hurt, and their lives have been changed, the pain can be very deep: so deep I would call them wounds of the soul. Not many people have experienced that level of pain.

Try to remember your child is the same, incredibly unique, gifted, and talented person they were before the incident or rough patch they have gone through. They have been through something hard, which is the unfortunate side of the human experience. As their parent, you can help them work through the grief, the guilt, and the tears and have an opportunity to teach them that their value runs deeper than their mistakes or what could have simply been an accident.

That time of healing becomes a gift to them; please don't let the incident define your child for the rest of their lives. Sure, people know. They are talking and judging, but if you are careful not to shame your child and to focus on healing, one day, they will possess a greater level of wisdom and insight. Deep suffering brings understanding, as hard as it is to live through, and if we are careful not to let the tragedy define them, what they learn will be an instrument of healing for others. But, it takes time, a lot of support, and compassion for both you and your child to get to solid ground again.

- 'Who are the like-minded parents in my life?'

- 'What is my child's greatest character trait?'

- 'Who can I bring in to help develop that gift in my child?'

- 'Have I taken the time to cry and heal?'

JOURNAL

What or who is defining who I am? What's been my 'security blanket'?

Do I have unhealthy expectations of a spouse? Like Jerry Maguire, am I expecting them to complete me?

Am I expecting my children's accomplishments to boost how I feel about myself?

What is in front of me? What or who is left?

Please visit www.crushedwhenparentingishard.com to receive free printable journal pages featuring the art of Emily Dayton.

Crushed

"Your heart is greater than your wounds."—Henri Nouwen

Regardless of what situation has left you crushed, there are very real reasons you feel the way you do. When life blindsides you, the expectations and vision of what you thought life was are blown out of the water. What you're left with is a lot of questions of what you thought to be true. Questioning is normal. Understand that being shaken is not a weakness. Disappointments and struggles are a part of life.

Some people are left with a strong feeling of lack of control and want to fix things right away. Part of why I say, 'navigating out of a situation,' so much is because that questioning of, 'where we went wrong,' can be real emotional work to get yourself back to a place of security, but it's good work. It may just be that you didn't 'go wrong,' you simply missed a sign, or your child made a choice and did something wrong. I would caution you not to let the temptation to jump into 'batten down the hatches' forces of control with your child.

If you go full force making sure, 'no one gets out,' you could be doing more damage to yourself by stuffing the hurt emotions. Control is an illusion. It would have been easy to ground Andrew for a year and make him stay home, but he also would not have learned a thing and would have resented us deeply. Resentment leads to lack of respect, and he could have gone full force and done it again. We did not, and neither did he.

Darkness in life is nothing other than grief. It's important to notice grief and learn from it. Grief comes in many forms and is not only an emotion from an overwhelming tragedy. There are smaller situations that we experience through life that are 'mini-griefs.' Sometimes, they are secondary offshoots of a large loss; sometimes, they are just a part of the human experience. Life is good, life is beautiful, but it can also be very hard.

What I experienced in the aftermath of that night, I'm sure, was impacted by the seriousness of the deaths in our community. Had we not been on high alert already, I may have just told him he was stupid and moved on. I was consciously aware that my reaction to what happened was rooted in survivor's guilt. Why was I spared when other mothers were suffering boundless grief? There had to be meaning in the suffering, or I would lose my mind. No mother should have to live through this if there are ways we can be smart and proactive in prevention.

We want to teach our kids to be emotionally healthy; that has to come from us being strong. If we stuff our emotions and numb the pain, what we accumulate is bitterness and a hard heart. Most of what they learn is modeled by us. If the goal is for them to build resiliency, which every school tells us is a dire need, and we know they learn coping from us, we have a responsibility to work on ourselves so that they see us work through the 'mini-griefs.' They can watch us reach out to others—they can see us making an effort to be present, to pray, read, reflect, and exercise. They'll notice and know what to do when life hands them tough times. We fool ourselves and put our kids at a disadvantage when we cover up issues and don't allow the kids to see the process.

Grief has stages; what you may be experiencing is the bottom of the barrel and the stages before you could be overwhelming. It was for me—I held my breath for months.

For a very long time, when Andrew came home from school, my heart would flip in relief to see his face. That event with Andrew, combined with Emily juggling grief emotions with her need to be normal, go to school, and play soccer, it became clear we had no choice but to step back to stay grounded. Chip and I backing away from our extra commitments forced me to be very aware that I needed to be with my kids and nothing more. Eventually, I had to channel that energy into something positive for our family, or I would become bitter.

I've lived in the bottom of the pit; I know how it feels: 'What did we miss? Why can't I fix this?' Crises in family strip us down. What you have is a moment to pause and look at what part of your ego is being exposed. Recognizing what part of you has been hit is an opportunity for growth. Crisis hits our ego, and it hits our sense of confidence by drawing attention to our masks and camouflage. That can be a good thing. Recognize the chink in your armor, heal it, strengthen it, and move forward. The experience can be the beginning of some real growth.

One of my very closest friends was completely overwhelmed when her boys were little. She described having three young under six as feeling like she was underwater with just her nose above the surface. I've noticed many parents feel that way with their big kid's situation. It can feel heavy and desperate, as if you are standing on your toes in the waves, keeping your head out and trying to breathe.

Some situations can feel stifling and stop us in our tracks. Some days, it's hard just to open your eyes, let alone get out of bed. There is a chance that things are so dark and desolate that you might be dealing with a situational depression. Darkness came be overwhelming, and we want to run and numb. Please, don't. If you think you are in such a place, please reach out to someone for help and build up your reinforcements while you heal.

In ancient times, it's said that if a pot broke, they wouldn't throw out the pot. They would repair the pot and seal it with gold. The end result is a piece of pottery, lined with gold, cracks still showing, gold peeking through, and that's the beautiful part of wisdom. Wisdom, really, is healed pain.

When your expectations of life, as you know it, are hit hard, you experience real pain. You aren't imagining it. You aren't weak, and you don't need to 'pull it together,' 'suck it up,' or 'get over it.' Right now, your 'cloud' doesn't seem to have a 'silver lining,' and it doesn't seem to be 'working itself all out in the end.' For now, this is what you're living in, and it may not go away. This could be your new normal. It's normal to get annoyed when people say, 'It's all good,' because, honestly, what you're going through is not. That does not mean good won't come from it, but right now, it sucks. You are allowed to take the time to understand why you feel the way you do so you can restructure and plant your feet again on solid ground. That takes time.

Finding a Healthy Sense of Self

So, where does all the disappointment of unmet expectations come from? Remember that exposed ego? It comes from there, our sense of self and how we define ourselves. I do think there are levels of maturity when we talk about ego. I don't mean a big, narcissistic ego, full of conceit or an inflated image of who you are. When I say ego, I mean ego in its truest sense. I'm talking about your emotional security and where it's rooted. All of us have parts of us that have a healthy self-worth, and all of us have a tendency to cling to external definitions for confidence.

We all have a basic need for security emotionally. If we had a perfectly formed experience as children, we would understand that our value is in who we are, that we are a child of God, and our gifts and talents are an irreplaceable, valuable piece in the lives of others. But, no one had a perfect emotional formation. Some did better than others, but we all have weaknesses and insecurities. In our imperfection, most of us cling to exterior markers that we identify so closely with that, sometimes, they become WHO we are.

In our culture, it is easy to have our confidence and sense of self rooted in finances, people, or in status. If our security is found in finances, then we will do everything we can to make sure we are financially sound. We proudly display our house, community, car, and bank roll. For some people, the need for power and control is their self worth and motivation for every move they make. They are in charge, and when things get bad, they are REALLY in charge, micromanaging EVERYTHING and EVERYONE. When our confidence is grounded in things that can be removed and when those things we hang onto are taken away, so is our identity.

If we depend on relationships alone, then our identity is molded by who we are with. Apart from our relationships, our self worth struggles. Some even take on the persona of whom they are attempting to fill their insecurity with. This is common in teens who are trying to discover who they are.

As an adult, it's a lot of pressure to expect our emotional well-being to be satisfied by a spouse, excelling kids, and doting friends. If people become our identity: 'I am Emily's mom' 'I am Chip's wife,' not, 'I am Melissa, a person deeply committed to helping others find peace and healing,' we lose the essence of who we are. We lose our self worth when they don't approve of our decisions or lifestyle. Some people desperately need attention and validation from others. To them, those affirmations prove they have value. The need to be held in high regard, and if not, they crumble.

Spouses struggle with this when one is desperately trying to 'fix' the situation, and the other has thrown in the towel. Or, they desperately WANT the spouse to fix it, and they just can't. It's hard when we feel we have failed at achieving a goal or part of the life we thought. But, it's not the end; life continues. The sun still comes up, regardless of you wanting it to, every day. And, every day brings opportunities for grace, if we look for it.

That deep, basic need for affection, rooted in all of us, cannot be filled by things or the love of others. It can, ultimately, only be found in God. I say that because, regardless of what you believe, deep within each of us is a need for affection, affirmation, and the desire to know we are valuable beyond the surface. We all want to be deeply and unconditionally loved. When we expect people, who are miserably flawed, to love us perfectly, we will always be disappointed.

We put exhaustive pressure on others when we expect them to fulfill all our emotional needs. When things in life are dark, that pressure can be unrealistic. The result is we feel alone in the battle: rejected, isolated, and maybe even abandoned because there is no way they can fill that hole. To gain strength, we need to find a deeper meaning, purpose, power faith in something bigger than ourselves.

One of the most helpful phrases I heard during my time of healing was from one of my wise teachers. She shared a reflection on the phrase, 'We had hoped.' There is so much depth of life in that one statement. People disappoint, but God gently shows the way to healing. I found reflecting and praying on that phrased a point of growth. The phrase helped me see through the emotions, look at the bigger picture, and let the disappointments go.

More Layers

About a year and a half after the cluster began, the golf course that my husband worked at was closed by the government. The BRAC was responsible for many army base closures across the country. We knew it was coming, but we weren't worried. Chip had won awards for the work that he had done at the golf course, and everyone who worked for him adored him. He was offered a couple of jobs before the closing and had many friends working at other golf courses. We never thought that he wouldn't get another job right away.

While we have work full-time with the organization, it's still been a very long four years, and he still doesn't have the job that we thought he would have by now. Losing that financial security really made us focus on our goals as a family and what kind of life we wanted for them.

Between the hurricane and the golf course closing, we not only experienced more burdens but also gained a newfound understanding of how some struggle to simply eat, keep the lights on, and survive their whole lives on not quite enough. It has been an eye opener, for sure, and a very real experience of stripping down of those extra securities. But, it has also been a great lesson in simplicity, compassion, and empathy.

Those lessons are invaluable to the work we do with a very real understanding that the reality of life is hard. Sometimes, no matter what efforts you make, burdens remain. The best and only thing we can do is learn to be grateful and live every day to the best of our ability, focused on what is truly valuable in life.

Other people may make snide remarks about your situation without empathy, assuming all sorts of things they think you have or have not done. Those remarks CAN'T matter. Unless someone has lived what you're living and has been with you side-by-side every minute, they don't know how heavy your burden is. It doesn't matter what their perception is, keep moving forward.

With our securities were stripped away, the kids were who we had left to focus on. You don't need money to have good relationships. I don't want to miss my kids growing up because I was stuck in a place of fear, and I don't want their emotional securities damaged because I lived life in a tunnel. By living each day and being present in each moment with the kids, we have grown stronger as a family.

Finding Light

Pain is real. People are important, and kindness and compassion trump everything when we are tuned into others. Self-worth has absolutely nothing to do with what we own, where we live, or how perfect our life appears from the outside. Our purpose in life comes from impacting others, and pain can be relieved by doing so, acts of kindness could be your glimmer of light.

If you look at some of the great masters, the great artists, like Rembrandt, at first, those paintings are black. They're really dark, and they're ugly. The beautiful thing about some of those old paintings, though, is they're really a study of light, which is so funny because most of the canvas is black. If you start to study them and notice the subtleties, however, you can see the very faint touches of light on the side of a face, on an arm, on a sleeve, or a piece of fabric. You start to notice the smaller things you could have missed. You would have never seen that gentle light if it was not for the contrast to the darkness.

There is always some light. Even in the darkest times, there is always something that you can find to hold onto and give you hope. In a crisis, there are helpers, reminders of good in the world. One of the greatest things you can learn when you've been stripped down to nothing is that what's left in front of you is often what's most valuable. We saw it in the people who came together in the cluster, we saw it after the hurricane, you can find it too.

If life has stripped you down to nothing, what do you have left? That's what is most important.

Start there. Begin again. **What's left is where you need to focus.**

- 'What or who is defining who I am? What's been my 'security blanket?"

- 'Do I have unhealthy expectations of a spouse? Like Jerry Maguire, am I expecting them to complete me?'

- 'Am I expecting my children's accomplishments to boost how I feel about myself?'

- 'What is in front of me? What or who is left?'

JOURNAL

Has shame and/or fear been under your reactions to your family's situation?

What's under the shame and fear?

Have you tried to reflect with empathy on how your child feels?

How could you respond with compassion?

Please visit www.crushedwhenparentingishard.com to receive free printable journal pages featuring the art of Emily Dayton.

Unfulfilled Expectations

"People are disturbed not by things, but by the view they take of them."—Epictetus

Over the course of four years, Chip and I have met many parents who loved their children, had strong family bonds, and it still wasn't enough to spare them from heartache. Sadness and hardships are an unfortunate element of the human existence. Our hearts break for them, especially when they feel that they weren't enough or missed something. That is a hard burden to carry.

But we also have met parents that are having trouble and really don't know which end is up or where to start. For them, we give referrals to help they'll need but we also suggest some self reflection, which is something we all need to do on a regular basis, for personal growth. Working on ourselves, regardless of how strong we are, will always be a benefit to the people around us. When are kids are hurting, even more so. Understanding the conflict is important, understanding why you react the way you do is a deeper reflection. Your expectations in life are connected to how you will respond.

There are aspects of mental health and addiction that need to have professional treatment. But the question we get often from parents is 'What do we do in between those counseling sessions?' Whether your child is doing that hard work of learning to live with their diagnosis or you teen is simply rebelling and you feel out of control, there are things you can personally work on that will make a difference. One of those things is your motivation in parenting. Even the best parents need to be continually evaluating if they are parenting from a place of strength or weakness. Are our motivations about us, or our child? It's a cyclical aspect of being a parent simply based on the organic, ever changing and moving parts of family life.

When parenting is new, it's easy to become absorbed with the physical aspect of caring for little children. Remember those babies that kept you up all night, teething, with earaches, the cold. Oh my gosh! That nose starts to run, and you panic because you know you won't sleep for the next week! It is exhausting, but there is some relief when our children get big enough to dress themselves, put their own shoes on, and become a little more independent. They, usually, can get themselves food, know what their homework is, and can take care of themselves. We seem to be under this misconception that when they get older, it gets easier. Then, the teen years hit.

As teens start to develop and establish their own independence, we watch them soar in their activities and the things they love. There are moments that our hearts will remember for life, proud moments and milestones that shape them into the adult they are becoming. But, with that extra independence can come difficulties in family. There is driving, new friendships and experiences, other families with different rules, and the list goes on. Most conflicts are growing pains; some are greater and take more time to work out.

Of course, the level of difficulty with our teens depends on many factors, including their temperament and personality. Honestly, some kids are just easier than others and have less defiance in them. Some are strong, pig-headed, and impulsive, which can put you into defensive mode pretty quickly. Frustrating as that may be, we don't, necessarily, want a kid who is so passive there are never any issues. We want them to have some inner strength and will that is synonymous with resiliency.

I found my teens that are closest to me, emotionally, sometimes have a hard time breaking away. They almost look for conflict, so they can 'hate me.' Hating me makes the inevitable separation easier to handle. It doesn't mean I tolerate bad behavior, but it does mean I'm careful with my response. Understanding where the head-butting is coming from helps with how we react to a 'phase.'

Teens that are disruptive as they establish new independence because they are making it easier to remove themselves from you is one category. Teens who are pushing the envelope by taking major risks, while being disobedient, is a discipline issue. When you are fighting addiction as your obstacle, there is a whole other layer. Addiction leaves you dealing with a child who is not making choices reflective of your parenting. That is the stigma surrounding families I wish we could eliminate. Either way, it is essential that clearly-defined boundaries are set, and consequences are laid out before an issue pops up. For parents, the hardest part is always enforcing those consequences; we need to be ready to do that work.

Outside Influences: Problems come up when easily-influenced teens are looking for 'family' in other people. Who your kids surround themselves with, can impact your relationship with them, and not always for better. If they are making bad choices and bonding with a friend group that is no good for them, conflicts can fly. That draw to others can be from rebellion, low self-esteem, or lack of feeling 100% secure at home. That doesn't mean that they are not loved or in a secure home; it could just be a combination of their temperament with their perceptions. Remember, their developing brain and reasoning aren't quite finished yet, which is why the utmost patience and inner strength are required for parents.

If you find you are running out of patience, that's when you look to your external supports to hold you up. Tough times are always an opportunity to teach and grow, but some cases are overwhelming and should not be lived through alone. Don't be afraid to reach out to people who may be able to help you through the situation before you become defeated. Sometimes, a rough spell like this becomes so complicated that it starts to impact other children in the family or even their marriages. So, don't wait until you're exhausted before you ask for help.

Expectations

We all have expectations for our kids' lives. We hope their high school experience is positive and pray that college is a place where they discover their path in life. When life doesn't go as planned, though, it takes some wrestling to work through those shattered expectations. And that's the nature of disappointments; they are wounds closely linked to the absence of what we had hoped. Sometimes, life just doesn't turn out the way we thought it would. We live in a pained world. People are wounded, and when they are, everyone they love is impacted.

Your expectations for your child can strongly impact how we work through family struggles. Remember, there is something unsettling about realizing you have no control over some of the things happening in their lives. We can be under a ton of pressure to 'fix' situations, so we don't interrupt their goals for the future. A family with a child who is having a really hard time navigating the transition from youth to adulthood needs to pause and try to make sense of the complexities. Pausing and changing direction takes time; there really is no easy fix.

Sometimes, as parents, we are left numb by the consequences of the decisions our children have made or, like we experienced with the cluster, circumstances that were happening in our community, which burden our own children. They were too young to navigate and understand what was happening. Add in a community of panicked adults, no outlet for healthy grieving, and there was added stress in our home. It really took some time to figure out the new normal of our daily life with the very real fear surrounding all of us.

I was traumatized, as well, from the alcohol poisoning incident with our son. I don't think I ever could have imagined that level of intensity when I pictured my children as teens. After a couple years, I realized I was spending a lot of my day holding my breath. When a family is living under high levels of stress for long periods of time, it isn't a healthy way to function, so once we're aware of it, we need to address it.

I spent a lot of time intentionally focused on bringing peace back to the house. For me, faith is my grounding force, so I upped my time in prayer and made sure I was meeting with my mentor. I also had some good books that I was reading for my heart to heal. The book of Psalms was a lifeline for me. There is not one human emotion that isn't represented in the Psalms, so I found great comfort there. Slowly, I began to breathe a bit easier, and my family felt the difference.

What's Your Filter?

Whether Catholicism is your tradition or not, Pope Francis is creating a stir because his focus is on healing the emotional and spiritual wounds of the culture with compassion. He says that we have to consider the Church a field hospital for those coming off of the battlefield. When I think of the culture that our kids are living in, they really are doing battle. Our kids are living a hard life with pressure and exposure to things above their maturity, compounded with the intensity of an often unattainable definition of success. They need many safe places: many field hospitals, not just our churches or our schools, but also our homes.

Our homes need to be that place where the kids come off the battlefield, heal their wounds, regain their footing, and be safe. They need to know they can come in and tell us anything, no matter how devastating and horrible, and we aren't going to shame them by reacting badly. Home is a place where they should be able to fail safely within the boundaries of family. If done well, we learn from our mistakes, so we can recover and move forward.

If home life is not lived with compassion, home can be a place that we are shamed and are left to battle a lifetime of feeling unworthy. Chip and I cringe when we hear a young person say, 'I could never tell my parents THAT; they said they'd kill me!' We know the parents didn't mean for them to feel that way, but some of them believe that's true. They fear the reaction far more than the fear of carrying a problem on their own. It's easier for them to go to friends who won't react, and in crisis, we need them to come to us. Please, remember, much of how we react to our kids in times of stress is due to our own expectations; make sure yours are healthy.

Getting our perceptions and expectations for our kids in line with a goal of a well-adjustment and emotional health is a good start. Being an emotionally strong adult with a healthy filter is key in how we react when things are hard. Taken to reflection: is the filter one of shame, or is it one of compassion? That doesn't mean you won't be disappointed, angry or hurt. It does mean you are committed to being the grown up and being a trusted person they can come to.

Old feelings of shame are often a place people react from when their expectations are not met. A big reaction often means a big old wound has been hit. The parent sees the unmet expectation as a lack of validation that they are doing well. That leaves them embarrassed and motivates them to not want that experience again. Shame, like fear, is quite a motivator but is an unhealthy approach. We have to face the disappointments in life head-on. You take a step forward by acknowledging where your reaction is coming from.

If you have crushed expectations that are about your self esteem, and you are shaming your child because you are disappointed, you could be doing some damage to your relationship. Shaming a child can be devastating to their self worth. Notice the nuance here, there is a healthy shame that helps to keep us in check: our conscience, which keeps us from breaking the law. A well formed conscience is a key element of healthy boundaries. It tells us that certain actions are wrong and that there's going to be negative consequences for making them.

Unhealthy shame says the person is bad, not the action is bad. Shame seen this way reflects that the person is a mistake, not the action. It is dangerous, corrosive and statistically leads to addiction, depression and suicide. Negative self-talk, "I'm bad," "I'm awful," "I'm not worth anything." As a parent, when things go wrong, there is a great temptation to shame a child because we're embarrassed and react because our expectations have not been met. We feel insecure that we haven't done the right job, and people might notice. It's much quicker to say, 'You dumb kid,' than 'That was a bad decision; let's do something about it.' Sometimes it is healthy to step away and stay silent to compose yourself so that you can respond well.

If your child comes home with a bad report card, or even arrested, how you react says it all. If your reaction to a situation is filled with yelling, "How could you do this to me? Our family? You need to get yourself together!" You teach them that your love of them is conditional and based on their performance. You teach them that you won't be there for them if they fail horribly, and they should not come to you in the future with a problem. Then, they'll build a wall: an emotional wall to make sure they don't get slammed again, making a hard situation worse. The unhealthy shame does damage.

We need to give ourselves some space to pause and recognize why we find ourselves reacting badly. If we want to take the opportunity to teach our children and have a transforming effect on them, we need to recognize what causes our big reactions. Recognizing the underlying layer of our emotions, and adjusting our needs, will help us respond in a better way.

As parents, we need to navigate from a place of strength versus a place of weakness that could do damage. That doesn't mean you won't be disappointed; it just means you're going to use the moment well. Anytime you have a consequence to a situation, you have an opportunity to teach. If you choose to build bridges by establishing you are a safe person who will help them through a tough time, you then become a trusted person when they really need it. You may not bail them out, but you will help them. You will build a stronger bond, and your child will gain some insight that they may have been closed to if you had shamed them.

Fear: If you live in fear that they will get hurt or make a bad choice, then your reactions will also be black and white. I have found that parents who navigate from a place of fear cause their kids to run and rebel. They tend to be authoritative and say no to pretty much everything without explanation or alternative. As parents, we have the right to say no when we feel, emotionally or physically, our kids may be in an unsafe place, but we need to look at why we feel the way we do. Parents of kids with addiction issues or other repetitive hard situations are coming from a different place of fear. Again, please rely on your external supports because your fear is real.

Instead of filtering what is happening in family through shame and fear, try to choose a filter of compassion and empathy. What happens when you choose to filter a situation through mercy, instead of shame? If you're not fluent in 'churchinese,' mercy is grace. Grace is a free gift. Mercy is sharing and understanding. It's empathy: "Yes, I remember pain like that." It's compassion: "I remember the person who helped me navigate through that, and I can do that with you." When we filter what's happened through grace and mercy, we turn that unhealthy shame, "You're bad," and transform it to, "That was bad." You transform from the parent who is frustrating their child by oppressing them and building walls to one who has become a 'wisdom person,' helping them grow.

When you can objectively look at a situation and say, "Alright, this is lousy. Let's navigate out of this. What are we going to learn from this?" and you work through it with them side-by-side, you learn as a family. Your relationship with your child builds. Creating memories is great, but real family bonds are formed through the tough stuff. It may take a while to step back and no longer react; you may need a timeout and some consult with another adult before you can sit with your child this way. But, the effort to do so will create a better place to work out what they are going through.

If you feel like you can't embrace your child in that safe place and use that filter, then you need to take a step back. Now, if you're a reactor parent, that means you should give yourself twenty-four hours before you address something, maybe longer to reflect on why you were hit so hard by the action—don't blast the kid as soon as they walk through the door. Take some time to really reflect and think, "How are we going to work through this? What's the lesson that can be learned here?"

If you're really angry, you've been living under stress, and your kid is repeatedly putting you through these situations where you just can't deal, I'm going to ask you to stop. I'm going to ask you to bring in your external support to help you with this child. Find a counselor, a mentor, a support system. These adults will help you as you work on yourself but can also be a strong asset to your child's growth. Sometimes you're too close to see the big picture, you need a buffer, as well as another adult to give your family a different perspective.

If it's not about us and our self-esteem when our kids excel, it's sometimes not about us when they are struggling. It's just life. Life isn't always an easy road or a road without potholes, so we need to stop placing ourselves and our kids under so much pressure to be perfect. You aren't a bad parent if your kid makes a stupid choice. You might need some work, though, if you make the stupid choice 'all about you' or look the other way, instead of using that moment to add value to their growth. Understanding our disappointment from our own expectations can give relief to hard situations.

Perceptions

Chip and I have close friends who have an autistic son that has a special place in our hearts; we just adore him. But, raising him has been a lot of work, sacrifice, and stress for them. We all need to honor and respect parents who live under constant stress like that and help them. We need to teach our children to have patience and compassion with special needs students they may know, too. Our friends asked us to attend a fundraiser dinner for their son's amazingly special school. At this event, a mother stood up to talk about her experience, parenting a child in the autistic spectrum, and how her perceptions changed after she worked through the disappointment of life that turned out in an unexpected way.

She began to tell a story about preparing her whole life for a trip to Rome. It was a place that she always wanted to go to. She planned and saved and dreamed about this trip her entire life. Finally, she was going to get to go. She was going to get to see the beautiful churches and cathedrals. She was going to be able to go to the Vatican and see the Pope at the window. She was going to be able to walk through the Sistine Chapel and see the incredible art that had been painted so long ago. The anticipation of that trip brought her joy every time she thought of it.

The woman continued, "Imagine you're finally on the plane for that flight, and mid-flight, the pilot says to you, 'Things are looking beautiful in Amsterdam,' and you say, 'Wait, I thought I was going to Rome.' Disappointed and frustrated, you wonder, 'Why are we going to Amsterdam?' 'I've been planning my whole life to go to Rome; this plane was going to Rome.' The plane lands, and you're disoriented, thinking, 'But, wait, this was not what I planned. How do I get to Rome?' You spend a lot of time fighting the reality that you're in Amsterdam when you really just want to be in Rome.

After some time, you finally look up and start to realize, 'I'm in Amsterdam, and it doesn't look like I'm leaving.' But, as you start to walk around the city, you recognize the beauty of the city. Journeying and walking around the town, you see the windmills and beautiful fields of tulips. While part of you still misses Rome because you never got to go there, you start to truly appreciate Amsterdam."

Parenting is a very real sacrifice of our own wants and needs. When life is hard, it can be the first time you truly understand what that means. How we view the situation can mean all the difference in beginning to move forward. I think that the story the mom told is a perfect example of our expectations not being met. Family, as we have experienced, is nothing like what we 'expected' as young parents; we have had to change our perceptions often. When you can see things from a new vantage point, it really does help you hit the redo button.

It's an easy trap to define your child's experience through your own and want certain things for them, but what we want for them may not be what they need to grow. They may not be able to fit the mold, and that might be a very good thing! But, when our expectations are not met, we question our purpose, and it may take a while to adjust to the new path you are on.

Most of us expect the path for our kids to be fairly straight forward: do well in school, be active, and participate. We're very much aware of that college application that's coming in just a couple short years, even if they aren't. When issues come up that start to really impact the family and disrupt the plan, we can get fearful or frustrated that they may not continue to fit that mold every kid 'needs' to fit into. We can start to white-knuckle raise our children by trying to control them, which creates more frustration, conflict, head-butting, and a lot of unhappiness.

Understanding Stress and Responses

Long periods of stress that don't seem to end can snowball and impact how we interpret situations that are happening in our life. That continual stress causes us to function in reaction mode, and some situations can transform from being simply being a cautious parent into white-knuckle parenting. A comparison of the impact of stress on our relationships was done by the University of Wisconsin-Madison. They conducted a study that discovered that parents with autistic children live under the same amount of stress as a combat soldier.[iii] *Any* person who lives under seemingly endless stress suffers in a similar way. That stress impacts has a physical impact on how we think and changes how we relate to others.

A good example of that study is found if you do an internet search of photographs featuring combat soldiers before, during, and after combat. What you can see in their faces is actually a change in the shape of their eyes and their expression. You can see the changes from the stress in their face before, during battle, as well as the lasting changes afterwards. That change you see is the physical impact of stress. Traumatic events do change us, recognizing why will help in healing those emotions.

All that stress clouds thinking and reasoning, like those times when someone confronts you, and you're left speechless but on the ride home, can think of 20 solid responses. Our ability to think clearly shuts down when the adrenaline from a 'fight-or-flight' response increases, causing us to clam up or react. Once the adrenaline disappears, you begin to think clearly. Your brain reacts the same way when your child hits you with news you aren't expecting or they do something uncharacteristically stupid. If you those high stress moments are continually, there is an impact on you physically.

Long periods of stress bring us back to our primal brain where we use old and possibly not the best patterns of reacting. Survival mode is meant to be protective; Cortisol is secreted when we're in high-stress situations and keeps us calm. This is okay temporarily, but can do damage long term. When that cortisol doesn't get a chance to dissipate, the build-up zaps the neurotransmitters responsible for our happiness and could leave us in a depression.

Recognizing stress has a physical impact is important not just for you, but for your child. By focusing on self-care, you can give yourself some breathing room. Exercise, prayer[iv], and meditation[v] have been proven to create space in thoughts and reduce stress levels. By reducing the cortisol, you'll allow space in your brain to think clearly.

But stuffing the stress can make your situation worse. Alcohol, drugs, and other numbing activities, like spending money or filling time, is simply going to stuff down the emotions causing the stress. If you are not addressing or aware of the importance of giving yourself relief, you could be causing a bitter cycle to begin.

When we ignore stress in our lives, we can get stuck in cycles of conflict with our family, causing big reactions, angry words, and people getting bitter and frustrated. Ignoring how you are reacting to stress is a contributor to building walls instead of bonds. Take time for yourself; give your brain relief by taking care of stress in a healthy way. When the stress is reduced and you are communicating better, you are modeling how to handle tough times, in a healthy way, to your child.

Facing the stress head on might seem overwhelming but physically, it's important to take care of yourself emotionally. There is a connection between our physical bodies and our emotions. A part of personal growth is recognizing that how you take care of yourself impacts your parenting, and attending to your 'whole self' will show in how you welcome your child when they come to you in a time of need.

Reevaluate expectations: Realize that most of us have a plan for our children to follow in life. Your plan may not happen. Deal with it. Deal with it quickly and now. The model and timeline for success that our culture puts in front of us doesn't have to be what we force our kids into. Children don't have to stay in the same school for four years; you can home school or find different, alternative schools. Some kids get a GED, move forward, and do great. Going against the stream doesn't mean they won't succeed. It means you chose their emotional well-being over other people's expectations.

If we're looking at a college student, they don't have to finish in four years or stay at the same school, either. They can take gap years, wait to start, and they can take a longer route. Every kid is different. They don't have to go away right out of high school into a fifty-thousand dollar a year school when they have no idea what they want to do. And, if they are struggling and hate being away, more so than that original adjustment as a freshman, bring them home and let them go to school locally. Why do we force them into situations that they aren't emotionally strong enough to handle?

Start looking at the individual child, not your plans, what their siblings did, and maybe not even the plan they have imposed on themselves. Often, we have a high achieving student who can't see beyond the culture's model of success. We need to give them space and permission to take a chance and try something different. We have to stop worrying about external expectations of what our kids are 'supposed' to be producing and reject the idea that our child is somehow successful when we get that beautiful sticker for the back of the car for the expensive school *we've* been saving their whole lives for them to go to.

Because what happens if they don't go? What happens if they don't get in? What happens if after hours of training, years with a soccer traveling team, and thousands of dollars you spent going to tournaments, they blow out their knee during their senior year and don't get the scholarship? Our culture measures our success by what we produce, but our children have to stop being defined by their performance.

Recognizing disappointment and readjusting expectations will help. If we don't, we fall into the danger of the 'cover up' when we feel inadequate or ashamed, and we try to make excuses. If we cover up the feelings, we create deeper issues. The stimulus for growth and change is to feel uncomfortable with the current situation. Give yourself permission to feel it. Use these opportunities of adversity for personal growth. If we numb, control, or make excuses, the issue remains, and shame prevails.

When you start to immerse yourself and commit yourself to those shifts in perceptions, the conversations with your child change and become more open. Your perceptions change and create a space where conflict is reduced. These changes in you begin to become noticeable to your family. When parents are grounded and have healthy expectations, the levels of stress deflate.

You can do hard things; done well, you will grow from them. You cannot pour from an empty cup, but what you can do is pour something toxic and damaging. No one mentions that, do they? It's human nature for our expectations to be about filling a hole in us, but when we adjust and see our expectations in a healthy way, we parent better. The shame and judgement we impart on them through embarrassment dissolves, and we begin to act with compassion. It's time to take off the Band-Aid.

If you feel like you don't have enough strength, remind yourself that the hard work will be worth it. Dig down deep and find the small burning ember, that tiny spark. Cradle it in both hands, pull it to your face, and gently blow. Do you see how the glow increases with just a small breath? Hold onto it, no matter how small. Be gentle—nurture that spark. Someday, it will grow so bright that the light will have no end. For now, remember that even the smallest flame can light a dark room.

'Shame is a soul eating emotion.'—CG Jung

- Has shame and/or fear been under your reactions to your family's situation?

- What's under the shame and fear?

- Have you tried to reflect with empathy on how your child feels?

- How could you respond with compassion?

JOURNAL

How do you see the business of life impacting your family?

List your commitments outside the home; what could you step back from?

How are you numbing yourself?

Are you using drugs and/or alcohol too much?

Please visit www.crushedwhenparentingishard.com to receive free printable journal pages featuring the art of Emily Dayton.

Control and Perfection Are Cover Ups

"I am careful not to confuse excellence with perfection. Excellence, I can reach for; perfection is God's business."—Michael J. Fox

No one likes to be uncomfortable; we spend our lives protecting ourselves from circumstances that will cause us pain, which is not very realistic. There can be an underlying stress, like a constant hum that keeps up, always watchful for a shoe to drop. That can be what life with a young person who is in an unpredictable or dangerous phase of life can feel like.

Stress is the space that's between our expectations of what life should be and the reality of what life truly is. It's the constant pull between what we think should be happening in our life and what is actually happening. The hum of stress becomes a reminder through all your waking hours that something isn't right, and that gnawing can keep us from focusing on what *is* right, which impacts how we relate to others. Attempts to control and suppress the hum, instead of facing it, keep us in an emotional prison of stress.

It is a prison we put ourselves in when we deny that our reality is not what it really is. People who get stuck controlling situations to run away from reality can be motivated by many things, but when it's our kids' lives that have put us there, two common motivators are shame and fear. No one enjoys the feelings of shame that show up when we feel we have failed as parents, and living under constant fear that harm will come your child's way can be exhausting. But trying to cover it up by pretending life is perfect can lead to defeat.

Our self defense mechanisms pushes us into denial, 'It's not really happening,' 'It's not such a big deal,' 'Everyone goes through hard times,' 'I can't change what's happening.' 'It's *ALL GOOD*': the great cover-up of our culture. That phrase, 'It's all good,' or 'Karma will take care of the wrongs,' is too commonly thrown out in response to someone sharing something hard. You may smile on the outside, but on the inside, you scream, 'It's not all good! It sucks! Karma? I didn't do anything to anyone!' It hurts. So, we put on a mask of perfectionism or we numb the emotions by filling every waking moment with a task that allows us to focus on anything other than the uncontrollable.

"People will do anything, no matter how absurd, to avoid facing their own souls."—C.G. Jung

Numbing fills our thoughts with anything we can to avoid what's happening; it's a natural response to painful situations. Being aware that we're doing it is the first step to peeling off the mask. Some people numb with business, some with drugs and alcohol. We are seeing escalating trends of opiate use. Consider this: the United States is only 5% of the world's population, yet we consume 80% of the entire world's pain medications. That, to me, says far more about emotional pain and numbing than it does physical pain.

Those who are perfectionist overcommit to numb by joining committees, planning events, volunteering, and being so very busy that they don't have to think about anything uncomfortable or any inadequacy at home. They live their own lives, proving their worth, based on the affirmation and accolades of others.

Then, following suit, the perfectionist over-schedules their kids, hoping again that the perfect 'successful' child will fulfill their meaning in life and erase feelings of inadequacy. We want them to be the best of the best. We push them to have the 4.0. We push them to be the president of this, the president of that, the captain of the varsity teams. If everything is perfect, then no one will know. It's the big cover up.

When Emily and Andrew were in high school, I couldn't control what was happening around them, so my method was to submerse myself in studying and reading. Now, the end result was good; I learned a great amount about the teen brain, substance abuse, and mental health, but I'm not so sure I was finding relief for that hum of stress. The hours of reading and googling left me with some significant wrinkles—one was so big that my then-2-year-old tried to wipe it off my forehead with a baby wipe, saying 'boo-boo.'

Sometimes, we're overtly controlling. We're making sure our house is in order and designed to perfection with perfect landscaping and curb appeal. The car we drive and the technology we use is the best. We're making sure that our clothes and home interior are up to date with current designs. Our kids are signed up for the best activities with the most expensive rates. We drive our kid, whether they want to go or not. From the outside, life is perfect. We're making sure that 'all our ducks are in a row' but it is all just a big cover up.

Sometimes, the control is more passive, emotional, and manipulative. If we can control reactions, actions, and others, nothing will increase the fear or shame in us. It is so much easier to point out the flaws in others than ourselves. I would have to caution that passive-aggressive control can be really damaging to relationships with your children. It is a corrosive relationship that plays with other people as pawns. When young people are manipulated, their self-worth is being played with and we end up with an insecure adult with an inability to say no when needed.

Passive-aggressive manipulation is confusing for a young person. Parents are supposed to be a rock or sure foundation that keeps kids grounded as they grow. Manipulation through guilt or fear is an unpredictable emotional response. Unpredictable responses make adults that are hard to read, and boundaries and limits are confused. Kids spend a lot of time wondering if you really mean what you are saying. They may get confused, trying to discern the layers and meaning, and they may, eventually, get so discouraged that they give up and build a wall to protect themselves.

Unpredictable adults that are navigating from a place of insecurity can cause kids to become confused and question their value because the adult's love is conditional and dependent on the child pleasing them. As adults, we don't want to defeat and shut down our teens. We shape how they see themselves and must be careful.

Especially in tough times, we need them to trust us enough to come to us, so we need to watch how we're interacting with our kids. There are some patterns that need to be taken to counseling. If you feel like you are overly controlling or suffering from perfectionism, that's something to bring to a 'wisdom person.'

Contentment in our life needs to come from a sense of emotional security, not external objects that can be taken away. Finding a deeper meaning, knowing you have a purpose beyond daily menial tasks means you are navigating from strength and not weakness. Again, for both Chip and I, the easy answer is faith: faith in a loving God, whose love is without condition and boundless in depth.

That kind of belief gives life meaning. It's a true sense of contentment to know, in your heart, you are created to be loved and have purpose. Faith means that, regardless of how deeply wounded your soul is, God is holding you and walking you through the trial, sending people your way who will help. If faith is not something you are comfortable with, please consider something. Don't define God by humans who failed to represent him well to you. Faith is a deeply personal and fulfilling journey— don't deny yourself that peace because someone hurt you.

We need to remember that our self-worth has to come from something bigger than external things. Our value isn't what we're producing; our value is rooted in the kind of person that we are. It's how we interact. If you're adding value every day to the people around you, then you're a highly successful person. I don't care what your bank account is. I don't care what your job is. If you're contributing to the lives of others, that's an incredible gift, and that's really what life's about.

Regardless of the hum, your focus is on moving forward. Too often, we rely on these external things that we control to make ourselves feel secure. When it's people we are relying on, like our spouses or kids, for our self-esteem, we will always be disappointed. People are flawed. People are limited. Other people can't be the only source of our fulfillment. Jerry Maguire was wrong; no one can complete you.

So, what do we do to readjust? Being aware of our need for control when we feel insecure is a point of pain but also a platform for healing and moving forward. Don't be afraid of what you'll uncover. When you take away the busy and take off the mask, you might find some ugly. That's ok. We all come to the table with our past relationship experience and our perceptions. We all have great memories, and we all have wounds.

Taking Time

Intentionally choose to simplify and reject the busy by peeling those layers and reevaluating your extra commitments. It is easy to think, "I could never quit the committee or the job. I've been the president of this or that for years. If I step away, it will fall apart." Remember, if something happened in your life and you ended up in the hospital, life would still move forward. All of those extra commitments would be taken care of by other people. Life would still happen; the sun would still rise, people would go to work. So, it's ok. Let go of those extras; your family needs you to be committed to working through the tough times.

Other people will stand up when you step back. That's exactly what we did and what happened. In the middle of the cluster, we needed to be a hundred percent with our kids. After we had that night with our Andrew, we stayed home even more. We wouldn't go out on the weekends. We would only go out for dinner during the week. If friends couldn't go out on a weeknight, we passed. We needed to be available for our family.

There have been articles, recently, about the argument for taking family leave when you have teenagers, and I would have to say there are times they really need you a whole lot more than they did when they were infants. If you want to have a greater influence on your kids than the outside world, you need to dig deep and strengthen those bonds, which takes time and intentional commitment.

Parents have the greatest impact on their kids, but if you feel like you have no control over your kids, that can be frightening. Focus on building bonds that are so strong that your influence is more profound than the enticement of the empty promises of the culture or a domineering group of friends making bad choices. The rebuilding takes intention and patience. Don't forget—you are the parent. You have every right to exercise your 'NO' when it's a matter of physical or emotional safety. But, remember how important it is to provide a safe alternative when you have a chance.

Notice the Culture

The culture that we're raising our children in is far more toxic than the one that we grew up in. We hear often from parents that teens are teens, and nothing's changed, or that we drank in high school. The problem with that statement is it ignores what they have exposure to. The alcohol is harder, the drugs stronger and deadly, and the promiscuity rampant. Boundaries and emotions are being hit hard. It is so much more than what we ever had. So, developmentally, they may be similar to who we were as teens, but what they have in front of them is far more dangerous.

It could be argued that social media and the cellphone have opened us up to a generation of kids that have been raised surrounded by pornography and many other things that would fall under the 'too much, too soon' category. Waiting until our kids get older and have the emotional security, maturity, and healthy relationships before they are introduced to such things has gotten away from us. Teens are under extreme pressure from parents and schools to perform, while, at the same time, given a 'free pass' to emotionally damaging activities. No one is immune to the impact of culture.

We are victims, like a frog in a pot. The story goes: If you put a frog into a pot of boiling water, it will jump out immediately. But, if you put that same frog in a pot of cold water and slowly simmer that pot to a boil, the frog will stay in that pot until it dies. That's how our culture has overtaken families. This is the world that our kids are growing up in, and as parents, we need to be tuned in to what they are exposed to, as a protective factor in their lives. Having eight kids, we have seen a HUGE difference between when our oldest was a teen and the life our teens are living now.

We can be fighting an uphill battle, as risk taking behaviors are glorified. At the same time, our kids could be numbing against the impossible. One feeds the other. No teen or young adult can achieve at the level the media, schools, and parents expect them to, perfectly. They are under a huge amount of pressure to earn the sticker on the back of the car for Mom and Dad, for school rankings, and peer competition; all while captaining the varsity team, being prom king or queen, and volunteering at the local soup kitchen. Our kids translate that unachievable pressure for perfection, which include the media's push for beauty, money, and power, into their achievements.

That sticker on the back of the car *can't* be the core of their self esteem. It's too easily taken away. They need to know that they, as well as all of us, are loved and accepted, regardless of what we're producing. It's a very difficult culture from the one we were raised in. We may not have control over what our kids have to live through, but we do have control over how we handle ourselves. By paying attention to our life choices, the pressure we put on them, how we deal with crises, we start to notice what kind of behavior we're modeling to our children. What we do is so much more powerful that what we say.

A Healthy Influence

Emily has said that when we took the time to walk her through the tough years, it helped her form a solid example for choosing healthy relationships and good friendships. At one point, we did pull her away from a toxic friend group. While she was angry at first, the extra time allowed her to readjust her compass. Overall, she is far happier in the long run with solid friendships and good people around her, and we are better for having such a close bond with her.

Your child needs that time with you. I used to sneak Emily out of school for some time alone, once in a while. We'd go out for lunch, get a manicure or a pedicure, and then pick up the little kids. She clung to those moments. They were lifelines for her. If I had been too busy, I wouldn't have noticed that she even needed them. Your interactions with your teenager or college student are fleeting; they're gone before you know it. You still have a profound impact on your kids as adults, but it's not the same. Take advantage of the time you have while they're in your house. Give them incredible gifts to move forward because life is not easy.

We fool ourselves, and we fool them if we think they're going to move on, go to college, graduate from college, get a job, and have a charmed life just because they went to the right school. Life is hard. People get sick. Bad things happen. Marriages break up. People lose their jobs. Life happens, and we want to build resiliency and give them coping skills to help them navigate those tough times.

Be Authentic—Take off the Mask and Show Them Who You Are

We have them for such a short time, and our influence is so profound. I think we need to remember that the formation of their character, their heart, how they love, and how they interact with other people is modeled after how we treat them and how we take care of them. Their self-worth needs to come from security in us and knowing, regardless of what happens that we're going to walk through it with them.

Our kids learn they have value by experiencing that they have purpose. Our role is not only to help them find that purpose for the future, but also to show them that they are valuable in the lives of others right now. Self esteem is built by doing and achieving, but parents often mistake a high GPA as the mark of a child who will be 'successful.' I don't mean we should encourage mediocrity. I mean we need to remember that the depth of a person's value is relational; it's found in impacting and interaction with others. That's not to say academic achievement won't help them make impacts in the future; we just need to remember the deeper core of who we are as people. The best way to show them this kind of value found in life is to model, in your own life, that people matter.

By modeling healthy healing, you'll show your kids that imperfections and wounds are a part of life. If we can heal our deep wounds, either from our childhood or from a broken marriage, if we can find a way to take off that Band-Aid and face the ugly, we can grow. You may be sad, exhausted, and deeply hurt, but as you work on forgiveness and unfulfilled expectations, you'll become better at seeing things on a deeper level. Your perceptions are going to change. Your interactions and how you treat your children are going to change, which can only benefit them. You can start to heal your relationship with them. It might sound overwhelming to do this personal self-work, but quite honestly, take baby steps: one thing at a time.

As you're working on yourself, if you can just change one thing you're doing with your child, the stress of that fear and shame will lessen. Any time Chip and I made a small adjustment, a small shift with one child that we were concerned over, we saw so much growth, in comparison to when we tried to control the situation. Try being attentive to eye contact and put the cell phone down when your kids are home. It's not that important. No one's that important. Say to yourself, "I'm going to make sure that we're having one meal a day at that table, whether it's breakfast, lunch, dinner, or even a snack after school."

You'll also notice that, as you ease up on controlling situations and walk away from perfection, you'll feel relief! The pressure that we put on ourselves to fit a mold is exhausting. Let what others think slide down your back. Take off the mask, be 100% authentic and real. It's the only way we'll be able to teach our kids to do the same. We have to model that healthy behavior so that they can be 100% themselves.

- How do you see the business of life impacting your family?

- List your commitments outside the home; what could you step back from?

- How are you numbing yourself?

- Are you using drugs and/or alcohol too much?

JOURNAL

Are you holding onto anger because you don't want the person to think the action is excusable?

Who would be free from the anger, if you forgive the person who wronged you?

Reflect on this statement: 'Unconditional love is not the same as unconditional acceptance.'

What is the connection between patience and being present?

Please visit www.crushedwhenparentingishard.com to receive free printable journal pages featuring the art of Emily Dayton.

Forgiveness and Patience

"Patience is power. Patience is not the absence of action; rather it is "timing". It waits on the right time to act, for the right principles and in the right way."—Fulton J. Sheen

There's a purification that happens if you navigate through darkness correctly without being bitter. You learn genuine humility. You learn compassion. You have empathy for others that you've never had before. One of the things that could happen when you're navigating your way out of darkness is that forgiveness rears its ugly head. You must forgive if you are not going to become bitter. Forgiveness is something that's really very difficult because I think, sometimes, we confuse forgiving someone with admitting that what they did wasn't so bad. I think we need to remember that forgiving someone absolutely doesn't say that. It just means that you're removing the shackles of the anger.

Forgiveness is hard. But, harboring injuries takes a lot of energy. Resisting a person or emotion exerts constant energy by thinking and holding onto wounds. The festering can destroy us and hence, our relationships, even the ones that are not in trouble. The anger towards a spouse or child that you harbor will be projected, in some way, onto the other people you are close to. It may come out as anger, control, or fear, but it will come out in a different way. To heal those wounds, we have to work through the process of forgiveness. It is work, and it is not easy.

Forgiveness is something that's very difficult because we confuse forgiving someone with approving of what they did, which would erase the wrong. The action or words were wrong; they caused pain. Yet, we harbor the hurt towards the person. You may never receive the apology you deserve. We need to remember that forgiving someone absolutely does not say that what they did was okay. It just means that you're willing to grow, move forward, and not live in the past.

The first step is accepting the truth of what's in front of you. There may not be a 'going back' to how things were. Lack of forgiveness is the fighting and resisting of that reality. That's hard, but honestly, if life's a journey, going backwards defeats the purpose, doesn't it? Moving forward requires we change our expectations and find a deepening of commitment to the end goal of stronger relationships. Instead of 'make it all go away,' we need to deeply understand the need to 'work through it' and be transformed to a person that sees life with a new perspective.

Acknowledging hurt is important, especially within family where wounds are deepest. There is an expectation that our loved ones will never hurt us, but they do. When you trust someone with your complete self, love them with all you have, and they betray you, intentionally or not, it hurts. Trust and security in those closest to us is shaken. It is easier to forgive an acquaintance or friend for a wrong than someone you are bonded to because the levels of trust are different.

When Andrew was angry with Emily after his night in the hospital, she was hurt. She couldn't figure out why he was mad at her for calling us because she wasn't tattling on him; she saved his life. She didn't realize, and probably, he didn't either, that it was much easier to blame her than to admit he really messed up. Finally, after about six weeks, we made them apologize to each other for the wrongs each of them felt and then hug, just like when they were little. They had to say 'I'm sorry. I love you, and I won't do that to you again.' It worked, mostly. Forgiveness takes time. Often, words spur the beginning of healing.

Forgiveness is a process of dying to those old expectations that our loved ones will love us perfectly. That wound can leave a feeling of abandonment, isolation, and confusion. But, you can use those feelings to find solid ground. Remember that expecting people to fulfill us perfectly emotionally is a misconception of human nature. The flaws in me must see the flaws in you, in addition to the great, and relent to the fact that bumps in the road will occur.

Pain is real. The wrong was real, and the confusion and disappointment that followed very real. But, the reality of personal growth is we learn more by navigating out of the chaos and disorder than easy times. If you are going to reconstruct or reorder your life and grow deeply from your experience, you must be intentional in the process. If you need someone to prop you up, find it. If you need interior support, pray through it. There are too many angry and bitter people in the world who are simply very wounded, hurt people that never healed. Please, don't be that person.

Words First and by Example

Forgiveness is important to model for your family. Something came up years ago when I was in a young mom's Bible study, and our conversations turned to how difficult it was to forgive. Unanimously, every single person agreed it was the most hard to do but that it was the one thing we all felt we needed to be able to do better. One of our friends was so moved from the conversation that the following week, she called women that she had teased in elementary school to apologize. It was a courageous and brave act on her part, and it was an act that was healing for her. But, her call was unimaginable healing for the receiver of that call. Now, I'm sure it brought out the pain and didn't fix what had happened, but hopefully, the apology gave permission to let go of some of it, once the anger subsided.

I also watched, a couple weeks later, another woman, at the beginning for the meeting, walk directly to her sister, hug her, and say 'I'm sorry—I love you.' I witnessed the end of an argument in a way I had personally never seen before. It was a witness to a courageous act of one sister to admit her love was greater than whatever their argument was, and a humbling sight to see her received openly even though the other's pain was tangible. At that moment, *it* was forgiven, and they moved forward.

The group decided, collectively, that we were going to commit to doing a better job at teaching our children forgiveness so that it wasn't for them as adults such a painful experience. We knew it meant we had to model the behavior. We would hold them accountable not only for their actions but also for accepting forgiveness and releasing the person from grudges. "I forgive you," would be added to our vocabulary.

We would also make sure we asked them to forgive us, if we did something wrong to them. That was empowering to the kids to see us humble ourselves like that. Admitting that you, as parents, are human and have feelings models the importance of understanding people sometimes hurt one another. We also committed to forgiving them when they had done something wrong to us or a sibling. The desire to stay connected is always more important than holding onto hurt feelings.

We all mess up. We all say things we shouldn't have said or do things that we shouldn't have done. But, we also need to let go of those hard moments to move forward. Forgiving someone does not mean what they did is excusable! It means you are freeing yourself and them from the anger that covers the pain. But it's a process, it takes time and commitment.

Apologizing is an act of humility, and often, it is poorly done and becomes an act of shaming, with added comments, like, "Don't do it again." We should teach openness to the apology. To be a true act of humility, forgiveness should be healing. We taught that the new response replaced "It's okay." Because we did this collectively, it became their normal.

My oldest son says that harboring anger is allowing a monster to live in your head. That is a great way to think about that negative spiral that happens when we refuse forgiveness. The monsters are walking through your head, and they've got big footprints. They can make a situation worse. They can make you very bitter, and resentment can grow, rather than finding healing. Remember that forgiving someone doesn't mean that what they did was right. It just means that your love for them is deeper than the anger.

The hard truth is people we love make choices, and their choices are not always good ones. We don't only suffer from our own mistakes; we suffer from others'. There are consequences that impact everyone. I call it, 'friendly fire,' when someone dear to you hurts you. When you love someone, you make the commitment to love them through these times. But, remember, unconditional love is not unconditional acceptance. You can love someone deeply but not love their choices. Clear boundaries and expectations are needed before, during, and after a crisis

Our response for the healing of our soul needs to be a sincere "I forgive you." Let go of the anger. If your child is repeatedly leaving you in a place of frustration and anger because of what you're going through, and you're pushing down hard on your child to apologize, "You need to apologize for what you've put us through," are you offering forgiveness in return? Are you saying the words, "I forgive you?" Or, is the repetition of the bad behavior causing resentment? I'm not suggesting we let that bad behavior go, but working through the hard times with a spirit of gentleness and empathy versus anger will produce more growth.

Trust

Forgiveness means you're willing to work on the relationship, that your commitment to the people you love is stronger than your pride or anger. Trust is the real issue. Just because someone apologizes to you does not mean they have re-earned trust. Trust of a lifetime can be washed away in just one act of betrayal. Trust is shattered when the betrayals are repeated over and over again. Enabling bad behavior is a weak pattern, so taking the time to create stronger patterns of love with boundaries is necessary. This can take a long time. Remember that commitment to wanting better and stronger relationships as your motivating force.

Use discernment and sound judgement, take one day at a time, and be gentle with yourself. Trust is the one thing that time can rebuild, though, in all honesty, it's the hardest. Time and consistency is essential in rebuilding trust, and if you are the one in charge, you can control a little bit more. If you're the one trying to earn it back, the same works, but you'll have to commit even harder to making sure you are consistently honest and living with integrity.

Trust is an important element in the self-esteem of our children, and self esteem is the core of resiliency and helping them choose the right path. That's why we put so much emphasis on letting go of old or unrealistic expectations. If your reaction is based on unfulfilled expectations, then there is a chance you are shaming them because your own self-worth was rocked. When a teen is living with an adult that reacts in a negative way, that's usually what's underneath. The unpredictability of an adult in actions or emotions leaves our kids in a defensive mode. They are trying to figure out if your actions match your words. Do you really mean it? Do you really love them, no matter what they have done?

Honesty is key. In our house, our children know if they are honest about a situation, they will get in far less trouble than if they lie their way out. Honesty breeds that predictability needed for trust between people. That's really hard with a young person struggling with addiction. Those external supports need to be heavily relied on, in that situation.

In our home, we feel so strongly about honesty that we won't let them lie if they don't want to play with a friend. We won't lie to them, and we won't lie to each other or outside our home. Honesty takes self-control and commitment, but I know too many parents who will return something at a store and lie as to why or lie to a doctor about finishing a medicine, even calling them 'white lies,' as if, somehow, integrity can be bent.

The truth is always the simplest; it creates an environment where excuses can't survive, and honest self-reflection is a must. There's no hiding or stuffing when you commit to being honest. Our children watch everything we do, even the small stuff. We must be as consistent as when they aren't around as we are in front of them. Honesty has to be modeled. They need to know omitting information is dishonest, as well. Leaving chunks out of a story is the same as lying. Your kids need to know that if they can't be 100% honest with you, you may not be able to help them if they are in trouble. If your kids are small, start practicing full disclosure now. They'll appreciate and trust you so much more as teens.

If the issue is between you and an older child, this can be a little challenging. They point out your failures immediately. If you have a child struggling with addiction, dishonesty is a part of the cycle. Stay strong with firm boundaries, discipline yourself to be consistent, and do not allow dishonest behavior or reward it. But, encourage them to be as honest as you are with them, so if they are in trouble, you are able to stand behind them and back them up. When they are open, even if you don't want to hear what they are going to say, praise them and show sincere gratitude for their honesty, not the behavior you're working to change. It's ok to be open about how the lying hurts and disappoints you.

Let's talk about spouses for a minute. Because we often get phone calls from people who are no longer married to their child's other parent, I'm very aware that the reality of 'co-parenting' and 'uncoupling' is not as smoothly done as some might want us to think. I want to challenge you to think back to when you were still in love with that person, when you did have a good relationship. Find your common ground, the point of connection, and hold onto it. You have a gift together: your child. Regardless of the pain, the bitterness, and the horrible things that may have happened, the love for your child has to be deeper than the anger that you might feel. It has to be.

If you're in a divorce situation, you can give a child a gift by forgiving the other parent for not effecting the expectations of the life you had hoped for. Forgiving them doesn't add validity to what happened; it helps you humbly move forward, in peace. It could take some time, work, and the wisdom of others, but if you intentionally choose to work on forgiveness as a process, your child benefits.

Your child feels the resentment; it makes them feel off-balance and unsure of where they came from. They are now living between you, literally. Whether you talk about the spouse in front of them or not, they know there is a divide. They are a piece of both of you. That resentment for the spouse carries over to the child, so you need to be very careful. Using your child as a sounding board for that anger is damaging to their wellbeing, so please, find a person who can help you to let go. Forgive. Write it down. Write down all the angry. Then, throw it out, burn it, toss it in the ocean, and don't look back.

Accepting forgiveness is sometimes harder than offering it. Self-shame is an awful pit, and if your anger is towards yourself, I'm going to ask you to take a moment and do an exercise. Take all those words the monsters in your head are saying to you, all the self-hate and failures, and write them down on paper in a column. In a second column next to the first, write the antonym. Get out the google machine, your phone, or a dictionary, and get to work on your new list.

Then, pause; notice the contrast. Then, fold your paper in between the two columns. Tear the page in half. Crumple the first list or tear it up. Take the new list of words and rewire your thinking. Take each word and write them on post-it notes. Put those where you can see them: in your car, on a mirror where you get dressed, or on your laptop. To go deeper, each day, in your journal, write one word at the top of the page. Look up the definition for the word, and write your thoughts on where you see that trait in you, even if it was in the past. Then, write where you can strive to reflect that trait during the day or week to come.

If you can't see 'beautiful' or 'wise' in yourself, write about a person who you do see those things in and express some gratitude for being able to recognize those qualities in that person. If you intentionally rewire your brain to a positive self-talk, you'll start to notice more joy markers, and you'll give your soul some relief. The only way to heal and grow is if you shift your thinking. The only way you can forgive is if you dig down deep to something bigger than yourself. Give yourself permission and the freedom to take the time to work through this. This work is hard, and it takes patience.

Patience is not passive. Patience is a teacher of humility and self-control. Developing patience is work, involving intentional pauses and choosing calm over chaos. A moment that is a teacher of patience can be God-sent, especially the hard-to-notice moments, which is why being intentional to work on how you react to a situation can be a rewarding and visible change of personal growth in you. Considering the hard times in life as gifts takes a shift in thinking, especially when waiting. Waiting is brutal. Remember, sometimes, God gives you opportunities for growth that come in packages you do not expect. Simplify and notice these triggers during the day, and you'll see the gift.

When we had only three children, Chip was working seven days a week. We had absolutely no money. Life was very stressful, and, to make things more complicated, our third child had a difficult transition into life with a bad first week in the NICU that followed us home. He was a hard baby, waking up five, six, seven times a night. He was very difficult during the day; there was lots of crying and being unsettled. It used to take two of us to change his diaper, and if Chip wasn't home, I needed a kid to help distract him. As he got older, he was constantly causing conflict. I had to keep him outside in a fenced-in yard or fenced park all the time because he had so much energy. He was really hard. I was exhausted. A mentor of mine said to me, "Melissa, you're not praying for patience, are you?"

I said, "Yes. I pray for patience all day long."

She said, "Stop! Stop praying for patience. God doesn't just give you patience. He *teaches* you patience! Pray for grace."

Of course, we had a chuckle, but it's true. Patience is learned through doing the hard work of waiting for life's shift in tides. It's a trick of presence that's hard when you are stuck in that stress of unmet expectations: what, in our minds, should be versus what our reality 'is.' That constant pull between the two can make you crazy. That pull is life, and eventually, we have to learn to exist in our expectations pulling against what our life actually is. That takes letting go of pride, ego, and control. For some people, patience is a real struggle.

Small efforts add up tremendously when you're trying to exercise patience. If you can learn through meditation, prayer, or simply practice to be present in the moment to the needs that need to be met or feelings experienced, you'll learn long-suffering patience and let go of that back-and-forth pull. Patience is the exercise of grace and perseverance. If we complain and are impatient in waiting, we do not experience personal growth.

What happens when we do the work, when we make small efforts in being present, is growth. The process of exercising patience in waiting, molds us, shapes us, and bends us. It's our choice, though, how we work through the process. We can work through waiting with spite, anger, and blame, leaving us bitter, or we can work through waiting and building patience with open eyes and minds to the lessons available for us. What we learn strengthens our resolve; we get better at waiting patiently because we see the benefit. But, what others see is a transformed, calmer person, and one that will have deep, compassionate humility. That kind of disposition becomes a gift to others.

Socks

I learned a tremendous amount of patience with that third child. I had to relearn self-control on a completely different level. He had a shoe issue, actually a sock issue, around 4 and 5 years old. If the seams were not exactly at the tips of his toes, he would freak out and rip his socks off and throw his shoes. If his laces were not precisely tightened with bows the exact size, he would kick his shoes off and throw said socks and shoes across the room, storming away. There was yelling by me and tears by all of us. We were perpetually late. I needed to help him figure this out. So, out comes the baby powder, a routine shake of the sock inside out, and then, turning it back to blow into it, making sure there weren't any pieces of imaginary anything. Then, we would begin. If one thing was out of place, BAM, tantrum.

I had to breathe through those tantrums over seams in socks rubbing his toes the wrong way. We got through half-hour long episodes to put shoes on. If I was not calm, he would not be calm. I needed to embrace that this child was having a hard time getting used to life, so out of necessity for survival, I became more patient. If I needed to sit on the floor with him for twenty-five minutes, sometimes, as he tied his shoes, adjusted seams, and made sure the bows were even, then I would. I needed to show him how to handle frustrations without yelling and kicking because he needed to learn that task, which was such a frustrating thing for him, could not create such an upheaval for the family.

The lesson for my older two kids was that when they were overwhelmed, I was willing to work and teach them. They learned firsthand that, as they watched the daily ordeal, that younger child needed more time, and they had to learn to wait. While they waited, they watched. When the episodes were over, I acknowledged their perseverance and kindness towards their little brother and thanked them. I also had their brother thank them for waiting. It was a very different experience than if I had been angry and yelled at all of them, trying to get out the door with everyone in tears. Because, honestly, there were mornings like that. I eventually had to be very organized and give myself the extra half hour to get them out the door in the mornings like this, until he figured it out. He did. But, to be honest, he still ties his shoes with even bows.

That presence I learned was incredibly helpful when the suicide cluster felt so endless. That stress of having no control or knowing if it was over put a lot of intensity in our decisions as parents, especially with discipline and how much freedom we were willing to give our kids. I had a dad say to me one time, 'Did you ever think you would think twice before disciplining a child because now the tracks were an option?' Yes, of course! We all did, at one time or another. It took a lot of patience and strength in us to be present in the moment and reasonable with our kids so we weren't reacting and navigating from a place of fear. As silly as the sock story is, those months really did grow a great depth of patience in me that I never had before. I'm not sure I could have lived through the last 8 years without it.

When you have a child that you are working through a large issue with, it's not very different from the socks. They are having a hard time navigating life, and they are in need of an extra measure from you to teach and model healthy resiliency and coping skills. If you remind them, by your presence, that you will not abandon them, that you will not allow bad behavior, but you will help them through it, they will learn, as well as will other family members, that family sticks together through hard times.

It may seem the sock story is a ridiculous analogy for some of the situations you are in. I know some of you feel like you are wading through mud, and much more serious that a 4 year old's tantrum. But imagine you actually are wading in mud. There is no running through mud. You need to move slowly, you have no choice, and it's hard work that causes your muscles to burn. There are times you'll need to stop and take a deep breath before you continue moving forward.

It's the same effort with a seemingly never ending situation with your child, and you need to stop and slowly tackle one section at a time. If you can take those smaller difficult moments of not wanting to go to a counselor, school or countless other obstacles, and you can work through them one at a time with patience, you are building resiliency in yourself. If you can image how strong your legs will be once you're out of the mud, can you also imagine how resilient you and your child will be once your life calms down?

Patience is not a submissive virtue. Patience takes work. It's getting your ego in check. It's sacrificing that desire for an immediate response. It's reducing pride. It's a compassionate opening of your eyes to the wounds and the needs of others. Patience is waiting, and patience is revealing. It will show you where you still have work that needs to be done to remove your own selfishness. It shows you to be present and to live in each moment by growing empathy towards others and understanding that some things just take time.

Acceptance is learning to be present in each moment and trying not to think about that space between the reality and what you hoped. Instead, just be present where you are. Try and shift your focus off of your fears, past experiences, and work on providing emotional security to the people around you. Work on predictable responses; that are the kind of consistency that really matters. Patience means being aware of what's coming out of your mouth and not reacting badly. It means, taking the time to pause and to be an adult. Being patient is a selfless intention to add value and to know when to walk away and give someone time. Sometimes, we need to walk away and come back clear-minded so we don't respond in a reactive way that could do harm.

Patience understands that small shifts add up, and life's a marathon. It's a long run with life-teaching scenery along the way. Patience will build humility in you as you start to be present with the people around you. Humility, rooted in empathy and compassion, grows a heart of gentleness and true wisdom.

You know those people: the wise, calm, and deeply empathetic people who can simply sit with you when life is hard. They have that wisdom because they have learned it, most likely, through the hard lessons that they lived. When you start to soften and show that kind of goodness and gentleness towards other people, you start to see a softening in them. Those predictable responses that you're working on help others feel more secure, and you're actually giving them hope.

Waiting Can Be Brutal

When you are called to be patient with an adult child, there are more complexities added to the equation. A young adult has the means to walk away, whether justified or not, and it can break your heart. Sometimes, parents have to live with the absence of a child, not by their own choice. If a child chooses to remove themselves emotionally, it can be heart breaking for the family. But, they may need time to heal, get better, and grow. Possibly, that time away is an opportunity for other good people to influence them. Even knowing that the separation may not be permanent, loving them at a distance is a very hard patience to learn.

Their absence could be creating a space for you to notice the subtleties of what is happening. I want you to recognize the fact that the absence of them in the family is an opportunity to take the time to breathe. To be honest, it's partially a relief, don't feel guilty about that. The daily pull and stress of conflict and arguing is no longer there. You have time to pause, breathe, reflect and evaluate. Take this time to evaluate yourself, the bigger picture, and what your role is now in that older child's life. Focus on the good, what went right, and see if you can grow that connection with them. Hopefully in time your young person will return and be open to hearing your words. Make sure you are prepared with an authentic piece of yourself that is focused on your sincere desire for them as a person. Use the distance as an opportunity for growth.

For those of you who have a child that is distanced from you, either by choice or circumstance, I know you're in a stale, endless pain. Other people's comments, like, 'It takes time,' or, 'They'll come around,' do not help your grieving heart and regret. Acknowledge you are carrying a long-term stress right now and give yourself space for self-care. There times in life when a situation may seem endless, it's important that you don't become defeated.

It is sadly true that, sometimes, its years before an adult child will have that rock bottom moment or will soften enough to make progress in your relationship. For a parent, that waiting is very hard. Because the waiting seems endless, it is important to be aware of the frustration that goes along with long periods of time. Part of that frustration comes from your soul needing to see resolution. That might not be possible, immediately. Waiting patiently is exceptionally hard when you carry such a burden, but remember perseverance is learned through trial, and 'how' we choose to live as we move through each day. We can choose to live with regret and shame, or we can choose to find the hope in each day.

During your child's absence, try to create simple things in your life that you can see come to completion while you wait. As a form of self-care, focus on something other than your situation that adds value to your life and feeds your soul. A hobby, project, or volunteering can be healthy outlets and are not trivial. To begin building or creating something and seeing it to a finishing point brings an emotional reward. Carve some time to work on something that you can creatively mold and complete, something basic that doesn't add stress or more burden.

I know the rage right now is adult coloring books. Even though I am an artist, I, personally, can't stand them. People keep giving them to me, thinking I'll enjoy them, but I pass them to my kids, who love them. They place too much pressure to be perfect and stay in the lines. I would choose something else.

Make sure you find something that brings you satisfaction and joy. When you feel like you have no impact on a child, volunteering, and impacting others does help. Bringing someone a meal is easy; spending a day at a soup kitchen, buying some new clothes to donate to a shelter or foster children, raking an elderly person's yard, or walking their dog are all easy to complete. The effort will remind you that your impact is real, even if you child is rejecting you right now.

Other things you can try to help you move forward and take care of yourself are more personal. I want you to notice the good things. I want you to notice when you see a difference in yourself when you choose not to react but to respond. As you filter with compassion and empathy, what changes are you seeing? Then, write those small joys down. They're always there. Don't be afraid that it's going to take time. Part of the surrender of healing is acknowledging that you have no control, but remember, as you do this work, you are having a profound influence.

Simplify your life as much as possible. By persevering while waiting for a change, you will grow your emotional resiliency. It is easier to persevere through hard times when your life is not cluttered with extra commitments. The space you give yourself provides breathing room to you notice progress in yourself. Recognizing improvement builds strength and ultimately hope. Life won't seem as stagnant if you shift to notice the good things. Simplifying will help unearth the small joys, the bits of what your end goals for your family may be.

Space to grow is important; think of a potted plant.

A house plant can survive, even if you don't repot it, but it won't thrive. You could keep it alive for years with no growth. It won't bloom, and it may die. When you give those roots space, they grow to sustain the health of the plant. To break the cycle you are trying to rise above, you need to grow those roots deeper so you can bloom. That takes space, but it also requires leaving the old pot, having your existing roots ruffled, and a little extra TLC to make sure you survive the move to the larger pot. Picture that little plant in a bigger pot; it's kind of sad and awkward-looking. The plant takes a couple weeks to settle before you notice growth. So, create space in your calendar, in your brain, and in your soul to rest, breathe, and commit to doing the work to grow.

Allowing your family relationships and roots to honestly grow deeper is the hardest work you'll do together. Don't ignore that opportunity to recognize the need to use cover ups of control and perfection, or even shame. Let yourself feel uncomfortable, and do the hard work. The work will be the difference to being wiser, instead of bitter, in the end.

- Are you holding onto anger because you don't want the person to think the action is excusable?

- Who would be free from the anger, if you forgive the person who wronged you?

- Reflect on this statement: 'Unconditional love is not the same as unconditional acceptance.'

- What is the connection between patience and being present?

JOURNAL

Can you look up from focusing on what's wrong and notice the larger landscape of what's happening in your family? What is your #1 goal for your family? Make that your theme word.

Where do you find peace or rest for your soul? Take note of what you experience while you are there. Take a photo.

Find a photo of a happier/easier time and place it where you can see it everyday.

Find an inspirational quote book, the book of Psalm, or another book that you can take quotes from. Write one at a time and take the time to reflect on the quote.

Please visit www.crushedwhenparentingishard.com to receive free printable journal pages featuring the art of Emily Dayton.

Joy Markers

"It is during our darkest moments that we must focus on light."—Aristotle Onasis

After eight years from the first loss from our community, I can sincerely say I have the utmost respect for Lisa, Tim's mom, because what she has done in her grief is opening her heart for all to see. The sharing in her book is an honest and real depiction of their family's struggle, helping others see they are not alone. One of the stories Lisa tells is how another mom who also lost her son in the cluster saw her in the store one day not long after her son died. She noticed Lisa having a conversation and laughing. It was at that moment that she knew that life would move on, and she would be okay. Hope is found in small joys.

Those small joys can be lifelines on dark days. The small joys we miss because we're busy could be the path to our healing and growth; we need to see them, in order to benefit from them. In our culture that is full-steam-ahead to be 'successful,' powerful, beautiful, wealthy, etc., we have ourselves overcommitted to the point of insanity, and we're teaching our children this kind of pace is normal! It's not! Our souls are feeling it, and when life is hard, continuing to navigate at such a frantic pace is going to make your situation worse. Pope Benedict said that 'Success is not a virtue of God.' What he meant was the insanity of our culture's definition. We can have successful families, if the goal is true, deep contentment in life. It's time to simplify, step back, and give those roots time to settle in the new pot.

So, how do you move forward? Do you leave the old pot for the new? Take a moment and look at your life and how you spend your days. What healing moments is life giving you? Is there something that is a part of your routine or calendar that restores you? Keep that, grow that, and give yourself more time for that. In your day, what commitments are there that rob you, defeat you, and leave you exhausted? Would it be possible to step back? Can someone else take that from you?

Now, stop looking at the big, overwhelming picture of how far you have to go, and start noticing the small steps you're taking to get there. What's the very next thing you need to do? Focus on that. Do it well. Do it with compassion and kindness, even if it's uncomfortable. We have all had to call another parent and tell them something about their child they didn't want to hear or make an appointment at a place we dreaded going to. But, once you complete those tasks, you will relieve the stress of the anticipation of an awful experience, and quite often, those mini-accomplishments are good things, moments of grace and growth.

When you're going through a hard time with your kids, self-evaluation and these small things are important, not only because of the peace you'll gain, but also for the witness you're giving to your child. You're showing that you're committed to helping the family bonds grow, and you're willing to do the work. They may not let you know, but they are watching and can see a difference in you. It's time to be open and vulnerable, exposing your fears and hurt, as well as your genuine hopes. Holding onto the pride of 'successes' will simply be a wall for your kids. They, honestly, just want you, your unconditional love, and to trust that you will stand by them, no matter what. By being vulnerable and walking away from pride, you are showing them they are more important than money, power, or what others think.

You may be thinking, 'But, my kid just can't break this pattern.' Or, maybe you've lost a child, and you're clinging to your surviving children with white-knuckle fear. Finding hope is going to be a strong lifeline in your healing. If you want to protect them and build resiliency, then you have to dig deeper and ground your relationships with them. Taking the time to evaluate helps you see how the snowball of over commitment has affected you to be busy, stressed, and overworked. Busy is the cancerous thief of family life. Controlling them and every minute of your day isn't going to change the situation, and it may cause them to run from you, in self-defense. When times are hard, the space you create for yourself, in simplifying, allows you to notice the joys and move away from the fear.

Look Up

We are very fortunate to live so close to the ocean. When Chip and I run, we leave straight from the house, go one mile to the boards, through two miles of boardwalk, and then, return home. No complaints about the view, and it's nice and flat for our old bones. In the late fall and winter, it gets a little tricky because the winds pick up. Before we leave the house, we have to check our weather apps and see what direction the wind is coming from. That way, we make sure we run into the wind first so that it is at our back as we come home. The real tricky part starts when we begin to get snow.

The boardwalk is almost impossible to run on when it's covered with ice. It is a wise move to run down the center of the streets where the town crews have spread de-icer. One morning, we had just a dusting of snow, which can be slippery on the boards and more dangerous than a packed three inches. I was forced to look down the entire run to make sure I was planting my feet carefully where the wind had blown the snow away.

The whole time I was on the boardwalk, I keep fighting the urge to look up at the ocean because that's why we run on the boardwalk, to see the majesty and beauty of the sun rising over the water and the birds flying overhead. The temptation was palpable, and I kept sneaking peeks but would quickly return my eyes to my feet in front of me so that I didn't wipe out.

Finally, I was at the end of the boardwalk. Before I left to head home, I needed to have that one look. To do so, I had to stop running. I was able to look up at the waves as they crashed on the beach, the beautiful clouds that were forming in the sky, and the new sun that had just come over the horizon. That small moment restored my soul. But, to see the beauty, I had to STOP. LOOK UP and FOCUS to do so.

We experience times in life that are so overwhelming that we pinpoint our focus on what's going wrong, but that makes it almost impossible for us to look up and notice the beauty that surrounds us. That's not a fluffy statement. There is something in our human nature and the way our brains function that are actually drawn to the negative. Perhaps, it's one of those survival instincts to keep us from danger. By focusing on the positive and finding the small joys of life, though, we are rewiring our brains to be grateful, which has been found to change thought processes and increase happiness.

The hard experiences of life can change us for the worse, leaving us cynical and bitter. But, if we intentionally choose to shift focus to the good, we can create new paths through the hard times that can be transforming. Hardwire your brain to find the light, no matter how soft. Recognize in yourself that things are heavy and hard, but there is still good. Stop running. Stop trying to figure out where you're going to plant your feet and look up. However small, you need moments to hold onto and notice the beauty that surrounds you. Taking those moments in life that we're able to pause in the middle of conflict can bring us relief and great peace.

- Can you look up from focusing on what's wrong and notice the larger landscape of what's happening in your family? What is your #1 goal for your family? Make that your theme word.
- Where do you find peace or rest for your soul? Take note of what you experience while you are there. Take a photo.

- Find a photo of a happier/easier time and place it where you can see it everyday.
- Find an inspirational quote book, the book of Psalm, or another book that you can take quotes from. Write one at a time and take the time to reflect on the quote.

JOURNAL

Think of a time of day when you can take 15 minutes to pause and reflect. Schedule it into your day, even if you have to get up earlier.

Are you able to put that basket of rocks down and look up? What simple joys are in your day? Write on your phone, in a journal, on a Post-It, scrap of paper, blackboard in your kitchen a word, a phrase, a moment of joy, so you can remind yourself you've made it to a new place, even if it's just one step.

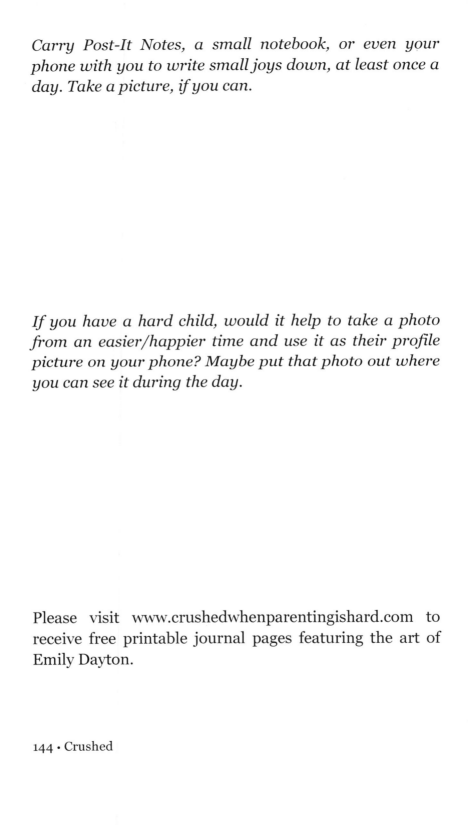

Carry Post-It Notes, a small notebook, or even your phone with you to write small joys down, at least once a day. Take a picture, if you can.

If you have a hard child, would it help to take a photo from an easier/happier time and use it as their profile picture on your phone? Maybe put that photo out where you can see it during the day.

Please visit www.crushedwhenparentingishard.com to receive free printable journal pages featuring the art of Emily Dayton.

Pausing Is a Gift

"Hope sees the invisible, feels the intangible and achieves the impossible."—Mother Teresa

This past December was tough; I was beginning to become overwhelmed that I was not going to be able to pull off Christmas as usual. From what I have learned, though, over the last 4 years, is that I need extra quiet and solitude to pray and reflect when things are feeling like a choke-hold.

One Saturday, a couple weeks before, it was a mild morning. I was up early, before the kids, as usual. I was going to sneak down to the boardwalk with my coffee and watch the sun come up. I went to the front door, and I heard little footsteps coming down behind me. Now, selfishly, I want this time to myself, but the little one who came down is number 7, my little Matthew. Most mornings, Matthew gets up before his eyes are open to watch ESPN and check the scores from the night before. He's done that since he was about three and a half. But, this morning, he looked at me, wide-eyed, and he asked, 'Where are you going?'

I sighed and told him I was going to watch the sunrise, took a deep breath, and made the time a gift to him, saying, 'Would you like to come?' He, of course, was thrilled. He put his coat and hat on, right over his pajamas, and hopped in the front seat of the car with me.

We got out of the car and sat down on the boardwalk, waiting for the sun to come up. Right before the sun rises, the sky's a lot brighter than you would expect, so we saw lots of beautiful oranges and reds. He was very excited with anticipation; it was his very first sunrise.

There's something incredibly valuable to one's soul that's found in a sunrise. The act of nature is never the same twice. Even if there are oppressive clouds in the sky, the sun usually finds its way to sneak through, even if just for a moment. The sunrise is a God given daily metaphor for hope and renewal.

Matthew cuddled up next to me on the bench, wiggling up in the crook of my arm like he's done since he was a baby, and we waited. Very slowly, the molten lava of the sun started to peek up over the horizon. It really was a spectacular sunrise that morning. There were just enough low-lying clouds that they picked up the beautiful, warm, pale yellow that was coming from the rays of the sun. There were, also, just enough clouds in the sky that were picking up some different colors yet still held the dark charcoal, almost purple color of the early morning.

I took a couple pictures of the sky, and then another couple pictures of Matthew sitting with me. It was a moment of pause. It was one of those moments that it didn't matter what was happening with the bank account. It didn't matter how many presents there would be under the tree. What mattered was our time with our family and making memories. I needed a little reminder. Christmas went just fine, and through some major juggling, close to acts of God, we pulled off a true Christmas miracle. We had a peaceful, joyful, and memorable holiday. It was one of our most sweet in 25 years.

I can't help but credit that sunrise morning for shifting my attitude. Moments like that have been lifelines through our last 8 years. Just like the pub markers and how Chip and I use what pregnancy or what child I was nursing as road markers for memories in our life, I want you to pause and notice these moments as markers in your life, too. Those moments of pause and reflection when we are able to notice those simple and small memories are powerful. When you take time to pause long enough to put down the basket of rocks and give yourself a moment to look up, you carve into your memory a gift. It becomes a joy marker.

The screensaver on my phone is from that morning. The photo is of Matthew, sitting on the bench, looking back over his shoulder at me with a sweet little smile, and red skies in front of him, waiting for the sun to rise. I see it each time I look at my phone. That image immediately brings me back to the incredible gratefulness I felt that morning with my sweet little Matthew on the boardwalk. Not only was it a gift to him, by my willingness to share my time with him but also, he and I now have a memory that he'll never forget: a moment that changed my whole demeanor and my outlook for what could have been a very hard holiday season.

Another trick and joy marker I use might help you. I have child who is in and out of the Mom Fan Club. At times, he hates me and can be a constant source of stress and conflict for the family. I know he'll grow out of it someday, but it is still hard. On my phone, I use a photo of him for his profile picture that was one of my favorites when he was 3 years old. That way, I am reminded when the phone rings or I get a text, to welcome whatever it is he's reaching out to me for with gentleness, instead of slapping him down. It reminds me to respond to him with a mother's love, not anger. That photo reminds me that I'm the adult and that he is still that small child and always will be in his heart, when he comes to me.

Patience was carved into my soul with that child. The photo I chose is him looking over his shoulder at me with a twinkle in his eye. As difficult as he was through those years, there was always a glimmer in his eye and a giggle that led to a deep belly laugh. He was the reason we 'had' to go out and play. He was the reason we have such great memories of playing with our kids, which began as desperate attempts to keep him occupied and have turned into full family soccer games when all the kids are home. Having him made us closer in a way. I want to make sure that I remember those memories, instead of remembering our conflicts. He's slowly growing up. Time will pass; he will continue to settle, and hopefully become the man we know he can be.

Being able to see hope is hard. I have had three women in my life through the years that were strong mentors to me who have taught me to do that. They provided for me a listening ear, a safe place to vent, and boundless wisdom. Sometimes, they would help by simply pointing to the good in a situation or the lesson that they saw. Find someone like that for yourself, someone who knows your heart. Tell them what you're working on, and ask them to help you notice the joy in the darkness.

Don't be too hard on yourself if you slip and have a day or two of wallowing and being overwhelmed. Henri Nouwen has a devotional book called *The Inner Voice of Love* where he talks about not being defeated in the journey. He says that being on the shoulder is much easier to put yourself back on the road than if you wandered off the road into a swamp. Writing the good down and meeting with a mentor will help you come back to the road when you slip off onto the shoulder.

- Think of a time of day when you can take 15 minutes to pause and reflect. Schedule it into your day, even if you have to get up earlier.

- Are you able to put that basket of rocks down and look up? What simple joys are in your day? Write on your phone, in a journal, on a post-it, scrap of paper, blackboard in your kitchen a word, a phrase, a moment of joy, so you can remind yourself you've made it to a new place, even if it's just one step.

- Carry Post-It Notes, a small notebook, or even your phone with you to write small joys down, at least once a day. Take a picture, if you can.

- If you have a hard child, would it help to take a photo from an easier/happier time and use it as their profile picture on your phone? Maybe put that photo out where you can see it during the day.

"Live your life each day as you would climb a mountain. An occasional glance towards the summit keeps the goal in mind, but many beautiful scenes are to be observed from each new vantage point."—Harold B. Melchart

JOURNAL

Make a date with your child. Don't talk about the issue; just enjoy each other. Practice listening, with eye contact. It's not easy. Try repeating what they have said, and ask if you heard them correctly. Respond with wisdom that adds value to the life of your child.

Please visit www.crushedwhenparentingishard.com to receive free printable journal pages featuring the art of Emily Dayton.

PART II

Building Trust

"An adult can have a PHd and the best training available, but if they do not have the trust of the young people, they are powerless."—Melissa Dayton

Moving forward with your teen, after you have taken a pause to heal yourself, check your motivations and expectations so you're ready to connect with them from a place of strength. When we start to change our perceptions and understand our teens better, we are on the road to rebuilding the trust that is so essential, not just for the teen years but also, for a lifetime of connection. Remember, while there are some situations you may not have control of, HOW you interact with your child will have a profound influence on the person they become. This involves, not only your interactions but also, what you will and will not allow; boundaries and discipline are important.

The Developing Brain

Discerning where your young person is coming from is important; this includes their temperament, social circles, cultural norms and trends, as well as their level of maturity. Developmentally, we need to understand their brain and the timing of a young person's reasoning. Our parents had no information about brain development; hormones were the excuse for every erratic behavior and bad decision. In the last 15 years, we've seen unbelievable development with the MRI[vi] and the ability to study the developing brain. What scientists have learned is that the last region of the brain to completely develop is the frontal lobe. The frontal lobe is responsible for reason, impulse control, and decision making.

That under-developed frontal lobe[vii], in no way, means that your child lacks intelligence. The reason that it takes so long for that frontal lobe to develop is because the brain is very busy strengthening other regions. It's a wonderful time to learn a language, math, to be an apprentice, or to learn a new skill. That's why, sometimes, we forget what we're walking into the kitchen for, but we can almost do the things we learned in high school and college without thinking. During the teenage years, the brain is actually carving paths, like walking through the woods, in your child's brain as they learn.

Understanding your teenager's brain development[viii] is important but is also helpful in resolving conflicts with them or helping them make decisions. Teens may be quick to react or clam up because they may not be able to articulate what they are really feeling or, more importantly, may be worried about disappointing you. The level of anger that they may be experiencing could be frustration covering up some pain. Our role is to help them peel those layers. Their perceptions are true to them, and we need to validate that we hear them, while understanding that they tend to be more black and white, as well as emotionally charged, which can cloud how they are feeling. Often, they make assumptions based on emotions, and when we calmly explain why we have chosen to make a decision and help them see our thought process, we are teaching them good reasoning skills.

Their level of brain development is why they seem to have their feet in two worlds, the adult world and the 10-year-old world. This is why we, sometimes, have incredible, deep conversations with them and proudly think, "This kid's going to change the world!" only to have them go into the other room and smack their younger brother for eating all the macaroni and cheese. There are days you may think, "My God, they will never be able to live outside the home." But, I promise you that their brain does come to completion at some point, and they are able to 'adult.'

Scientists say that around age 26 is when we can expect that the brain is fully developed.[viii] Again, that doesn't mean intelligence—it means processing speed. With our oldest son, we used that stat for a lot of fun and humor at the dinner table. We used to remind him, continually, that his clock was ticking, anytime he said something stupid. Even a week before his 26th birthday, I would yell at him, jokingly saying, 'But, you only have a week left, once that week is here, it's done, it's sealed—there's nothing else we can do, finished!' He would smirk. The final age of brain development is different for each person, although women or girls tend to be younger. There are even studies that are saying it never ends, which is good news for our son! Brain science is fascinating, and the developing brain is something all parents need to read about.

We gain more insight when we acknowledge the differences between the male and female brain. A male brain has less synapses between the two hemispheres of the brain, which means that a male is capable of removing the emotion from decisions, which, in some cases, is a real benefit, allowing them to be somewhat more objective than women. A woman's brain has the ability to switch back and forth between reasoning and emotion. The differences are good.

While it's easy to over-simplify the differences or get caught up in stereotypes, we have seen those differences in ourselves and our kids. In our school presentations, we use donuts as an example. A man will simply order which one he wants, while a woman will think of all the implications of her decision: 'I had sprinkles last time. I do like sour cream—maybe I'll get a Boston Crème.' While her male friend taps his foot, she laments to him that she's not sure if she will regret her decision of sprinkles versus no sprinkles. Silly as that is, it's a good example as to why teen boys are more impulsive. That impulsiveness in the teen years, combined with the underdeveloped frontal lobe, could lead them to risk-taking behaviors, some of which might be life-threatening. When our teens are learning to navigate life with a mental health or addiction issue, that impulsiveness can be frightening.

It's why there is so much emphasis on resiliency and coping skills. Many educators and counselors will tell us that those skills are in decline. Resiliency is built when they see they can recover from a failure. We want them to fail and experience consequences, so they can see they'll be ok if something goes wrong! But, we want that to happen in our line of vision, so we can help them. We have to stop protecting them from the uncomfortable, if we want them to build those skills. While a mental health condition is not a character flaw but a brain issue, we need to remember that traits, like perseverance, patience, and integrity, that we instill in our kids through conquering the smaller hard things, could be what helps them open up to an adult for help when they are dealing with a mental health crisis. Those strong traits help them through hard times, regardless of what they are.

Teen Brain and Substance Use

If you can see why teens need adults to guide them in their decision making and judgment on a regular day, *WHY* would we want them to impair their decision-making and impulse control at a greater level by allowing them to drink? We can no longer make the excuse, "We drank, too," with the information we now have. We know from our work in prevention that any contributing factor we can reduce improves the chances of saving a life. Drugs and alcohol are very common contributors.

Often, while I'm out and about, other parents will stop me to chat, so a trip to the food store can take a very long time. Many times, I have been stopped by a parent who starts to fill me in on what's happening with their young person. There have been times where I have to grip the shopping cart tightly and use every ounce of self-control not to reach out and smack the person I'm talking to.

Usually, the conversation ends up talking about how their kids drink, how they "know they do, but we drank when we were teenagers," "they're such good kids. They do well in school. They're successful on their sports team, and they have such nice friends. They all take care of each other, so I have no problem letting them drink at my house. I just take their keys."

Nothing makes me angrier, especially after we almost lost Andrew to alcohol poisoning. To claim, "We drank," giving ourselves permission to allow them to, is a lame excuse. When we drink alcohol, it immediately impacts our frontal lobe. Automatically, we think that we are capable of drinking more. Our inhibitions are lowered, we get a little louder, and we have conversations maybe we wouldn't have, if we hadn't had that drink. We relax, and maybe, we do a little dancing. For teenagers, they already have a slower-working frontal lobe when they're sober. When we add alcohol to the mix, we are allowing them to reduce their decision-making skills even more.

It's not just high school students at risk; we see this in colleges, as well. Binge drinking is a major issue, not just physically but also, emotionally. The first time away at school and trying new things can be attractive but can go too far. Just last year, we were on a prayer chain for a man who was a junior in college. He went out one night with his friends and just did too many shots. For a week, we prayed for him, and very sadly, he did not make it. 5,000 deaths a year are attributed to binge drinking. Alcohol still kills more people a year than drugs.

During the cluster, not everyone in our community reacted the same way. Some parents saw the substance connection but were so fearful that they decided allowing the drinking at their homes was the answer to keeping the kids safe. Almost every home, it seemed, was now permitting parties with the adults present. Many parents think that, by allowing teens to drink at home, a dangerous situation won't happen. But, statistically, we see that if you allow your children to drink at home, there's an 80% chance that they drink outside the home.

They won't fill you in on most of what happens while they're out, and we've heard plenty of stories about things from the kids that happened in basements while the parents were upstairs. Not too far from here, there was a young man who was invited to a small party with parents upstairs and a mixed group of older siblings' friends and his friends in the basement. The young man decided to snort a line of heroin for the first time and is now a quadriplegic that has to be cared for by his mother, 24 hours a day.

We also heard stories from young people who are allowed to go away for the weekend after prom and kids who destroyed the rental homes. One young lady, in particular, was date raped. She never told her parents because she wasn't supposed to be there. Two years later, she suffered from an eating disorder, and through intensive therapy, the parents discovered what happened that weekend. There are things that are happening that your kids aren't telling you about, and they're carrying those burdens with them. A snowball effect of all of those incidences could leave you with a child in a situational depression, and because they haven't told you about some of the things they've experimented with, you end up confused and not able to help them.

Marijuana has also changed drastically in the last 20 years; its THC levels are 80% stronger than when we were in high school and college. In a world that's so focused on success, getting into the right college, and having that high paying career, we can't downplay that regular pot smoking reduces kids' chances of graduating from college by 50% and can lower their IQ up to six points.[ix] Many kids are also taking their friends' study drugs, like Adderall, to give themselves an edge. Coming down from Adderall, one young adult in recovery told us, is like coming down off cocaine. He is certain that his opiate use began as a result of not being able to sleep from the drug.

Substance prevention is something that we touch on in our talks, especially drinking because of our own story, but we usually refer when we have a family that is desperately trying to help a young person with addiction. I have a friend Donna Destefano[x] from the prevention coalitions that I have served on who works tirelessly in the state. Her daughter and their family suffered with her recovery from a heroin addiction. Her message is that behind the most beautiful doors[xi], this opiate crisis exists. No one is immune. If this is your battle, you need people who have lived it to hold you up, please search them out.

Discipline and boundaries are also essential parts of parenting a teen. Clearly defined boundaries and consequences help provide that safe place to mess up. They know what to expect, and it may cause them to think twice before making an impulsive choice, which is why it is so important for you to be navigating from a place of strength, not fear or shame.

Never be embarrassed if your child has done something stupid or outrageous, even in public. ALL kids do stupid things, go somewhere they shouldn't, or try something that gets them into some kind of trouble. If not, they're with other kids who do. We did, and our parents did, too. It's the way of the teenager. It doesn't excuse the bad behavior, but 'pushing the envelope' is developmentally appropriate. It's why having rules and responsibilities at home is important. I would much rather they exercised their right to 'break the rules' over cleaning a bathroom than having no rules at home and looking elsewhere to push the envelope.

Try not to worry about what the gossip across town will say. Every town has them, and honestly, they just have nothing better to do with their time. Their opinion doesn't change your reality. Then, of course, there is the 'know-it-all parent' with the perfect child. Don't be fooled. They are simply masters of overlooking, ignoring, and allowing bad behavior so they don't have to discipline. Or, things have happened, and they have covered it up because, "What would the people at work say?"

Let your kids fail. Let them fail safely, break your rules and learn from the consequences. We need to use those opportunities for learning experiences, no sweep them under the rug. When parents don't allow their kids to feel the pain associated in the aftermath of bad behavior, the kids will continue to push the envelope, and they will have a mess of a high school experience on their hands. When we look the other way and miss opportunities to discipline and teach, the problem doesn't go away and will just rear its head at a later date in a bigger way.

It may be difficult to reinstate rules if you have had few, but if you have a young person who is not in a safe place, you need to have clearly defined limits for their safety and your sanity. If you have a teen that is having some 'growing' pains and pushing the boundaries, you need to be very clear as to what they are and what will happen when they are crossed. You also need to follow through.

That repetition will help rebuild a sense of order over time. Honestly, the earlier, the better, if you haven't done a good job establishing these markers.

Outside Help

If you have a young person that is depressed, abusing drugs and alcohol, or just not in a good place, reach out for help now. You are not a failure as a parent if you are looking to bring additional expertise into your lives. The sooner you ask, the sooner you can begin your journey towards healing. It's ok to recognize that you may need help establishing those supports emotionally and when needed to enforce consequences for your child. Many adults working together help create that safety net your family needs right now. If you are a single parent, you absolutely need backup for both you and your children. When we move from character development to safety, those supports are key.

Reach out to mentors and counselors, people who are willing to help guide you as you learn to navigate your unique situation and parent your child well. The coping skills that those external structures teach your child become the tools they need to recognize in themselves what triggers them to spiral, ways to cope, and when it's time ask for help. But just because others are helping you don't forget you are still a very important piece and influence in that process.

Sometimes I've seen parents assume that those external supports should naturally be the school system. They fall back on thinking all the answers should be found in that one spot, but, because of the number of students in a building that isn't always possible. We've heard parents expecting that the school needs to be solving all issues surrounding teen life. They are expecting the school to parent and be far more involved than they are equipped to be. Those expectations leaves them feeling frustrated and angry when they aren't fulfilled. We saw a little of that in the panic of our community, but we need to remember we're all imperfect and human, and with complex situations there has to be many players at the table to find a solution.

Parents can't forget they are an integral piece of the process, and schools need to remember their role in education needs carry over to parents, since they have access to information the parents do not. Often in the wake of a crisis in a school, mental health organizations will go into a school, provide grief counseling and train all the adults. Sometimes we assume everything has been taken care of and the problem solved.

While that process needs to happen, once those organizations leaves, the reality is, the work is just beginning. Sometimes adults aren't too sure what to do in the day-to-day, when there isn't a crisis. If we are committed to prevention, that's the time we have to intentionally implement strong coping and resiliency skills together, so that safety net for the kids. That net is built, piece by piece, step by step, in the small transactions of day to day living.

That's where our message of strengthening integrity, openness and communication to build a strong social structure with the school and community is important. ALL adults, the experts, the faculty and the parents need to work together. If adults are consistently modeling healthy communication and teamwork we will have an impact in their lives. The kids are watching and they can smell a faker a mile away. They know if there is infighting and inflamed egos, and it causes them to turn to each other instead of adults. They need to see us working together, not pointing fingers. We do this to keep them safe and so they trust us. Not just in times of crisis, but consistently through their journey.

Suffering is part of life the part of the human experience. None of us are perfect, and hardship can break us. Being cracked open allows us not only to see our flaws, but the flaws of others. That's a very real part of community. Being broken also allows life to reveal to us our undying need for others and that we can't do everything by ourselves. No one is perfect and no one is meant to live this life alone. We were born into community, and thrive when we have others to live life with. A strong community that pulls together in crisis creates positive memories for the kids in the wake of sadness. Social connection is so vital to us as humans, that without it, we fail to thrive. Its why isolation is a strong sign that someone is hurting, and why community is so essential to saving lives.

Stop Driving the Zamboni

Living in community means we share joys and we share burdens. But we have to do so in a healthy way without enabling bad patterns. We aren't meant to have all the answers or fix other people's problems. We are simply meant to be the best we can be for ourselves and others. Being emotionally grounded not only guards us from passing poor relationship patterns to young people but teaches kids how to handle life's ups and downs clearly.

It's important to reflect on how well you are modeling behavior to them. Are you showing them the joy markers of the lessons learned through pain? Or are you so afraid they will experience that pain, that you're trying to take it all away? Watching a child suffer is a very difficult thing to do and it so easy to take care of consequences for them so they don't have to feel that pain. No parent wants to see their child in a hard place.

I'm sure you have heard the term helicopter parent and how dangerous it is for them developmentally to orchestrate every minute of their day, not allowing them to make a decision on their own. We know that in the long term, it's better for kids to establish some independence by working on things themselves. Still, our shame and perfectionism cause us to hover. If you notice Helicopter parenting, it calls for a pause to take notice of the need for control and their expectations, and hopefully by now you've done that, if not go back are read chapters 5 & 6.

There is also a "Mower Parent" who runs ahead of their child removing any obstacles they may encounter. We have a new term for you—"Zamboni parent". A Zamboni parent dutifully trails behind the child erasing the consequences of every negative experience and consequence, trying to rescue the child from the pain of their mistakes. That parent is actually causes more damage by not allowing the child to live out the penalties associated with a bad choice.

When we go to schools we repeatedly hear from staff that there is a dire need for students to learn resiliency and coping skills. When we try to rescue them from experiencing negative consequences we are robbing from them the ability to build resiliency and coping skills by learning from their mistakes. They learn by that experience that failure happens, bad choices are made, but you can live through it. If you do 'your time' well, you'll learn something valuable about yourself and others in the process. One of my best examples of allowing one of my own child to fall is the story with my oldest son Christopher.

When Christopher was in college he signed up for too many extracurricular activities and on top of those clubs, decided that he would run for president of his sophomore class. I knew that there were a couple classes he wasn't doing very well in. I asked him not to run for office. Of Course he ignored me. A couple months later, he was elected president of his sophomore class.

The end of sophomore year he has failed two classes and was home with us for a semester. He was very angry, very angry with me, because the situation was in his mind, somehow his mother's fault. His attitude was bad, which added a lot of conflict to the family that very long semester. He learned going to community college for a term that he did not want to be home! He got his grades up and returned to finish college with his friends. Once there, he made sure failing did not happen again.

Christopher graduated with a political science major, was hired almost immediately out of college with a great job with the local representative. He was living a life making good money, collecting vineyard vines ties and enjoying the younger employees in local politics. Our arrangement was, one year at home so he could pay off student loans that he accumulated with the extra semester debacle, and then move on. He agreed and we expected him to hold up his end of the deal.

I started to notice that he was spending a lot of time with friends, going out at night, and his tie collection was growing. I reminded him, because I'm his mother, repeatedly of his student loans and why he was home with us. It started to become a real bone of contention between the two of us. I threw in a small 'rent' he had to pay to tighten his wallet, but that didn't work very well and he kept living large.

Then one day I went to get the mail, and at the top of the stack was this beautiful note on crane stationery, addressed to Christopher. I flipped over the envelope to see who was sending him such a lovely letter, and noticed it was from Brooks Brothers. That was the last straw for me, and I did what I never do, and opened his mail. What I found was a handwritten thank you note, from the salesman at Brooks Brothers for Christopher's recent purchase.

I lost my mind. Chip and I decided it was time to kick him out. There were the cries of pain from the extended family who thought we were being too hard on him, but we stood our ground. It was time for some tough love. In about a week he started packing his things and he started to move. So I said to him, 'You found a place to live?' And he replied 'Yes, I'm going to move in with my friend Adam from work'. I said 'Okay that's good, where will you be living?' He replied with a smirk on his face 'Well, we are going to be living in his parents' oceanfront house that's vacant because it's a summer home, and he's happy to have a roommate because he's lonely.' Not only did Christopher move to an oceanfront house, he ended up with a master suite, and the mother of his friend decided there was not much chance they would clean her house, so she hired them a cleaning woman!

My plan seemed to fail, but it was an important piece to the puzzle that led to his crash and burn which brought him ultimately to making the best decision of his life. And the student loans . . . are still on hold until school is over. So the consequences did not disappear they are just delayed, he still has to face them. But Chip and I don't own that, he does.

In the great scheme of things he still learned a very valuable lesson and so did we. Parents sometimes have to do hard things for the benefit of the child. By putting a foot down and establishing a healthy boundary, we allow them to experience the consequences of their choices. We give them the gift of ownership.

Eventually, the stress of living a life that conflicted with his core values caught up with him. He came home one day almost a year later and confessed to Chip and I that he was miserable, had grey hair and was drinking antacid for lunch. Politics had taken its toll on his 24 year old body and soul. He decided to quit and returned home, far more humble than he left.

Shortly after Hurricane Sandy hit, he helped us volunteer in the community and found that serving others was adding back into his life what was missing. He began meeting with an old high school teacher who was about to become a priest, for weekly spiritual direction about his path in life. By the following fall, he realized a lifelong call, and entered Seminary. He now is the happiest, most complete and content he has ever been in his life. It came from living through a struggle, that we had to stand back and allow to happen, which wasn't easy.

Let go of the wheel of the Zamboni. It's just another parent crutch to avoid pain. It is easier for YOU when you fix a situation for them! But not for them in the long run, it just delays important life lessons they need to learn. To build resiliency we need to allow them to fail, and do so within the safety net of family, which is easier while they still live at home.

Allowing them to go through these trials at home, they learn that they can stand on their own two feet and that humility and asking for forgiveness is a strong character trait that will take them far. They learn that they do have the tools to navigate out of a situation as messy as it might be, and to avoid making impulsive decisions that will have negative consequences in the future.

If your child ever does end up in a serious crisis, they will that have resiliency built into them. That resiliency may not remove the crisis, but they'll maneuver through it a little stronger. They will understand that hard times can be, they are temporary. And, if done with care, they learn that you will stand by them as they climb out of the rough spot.

We don't want them to go off to college for the first time and fail for the first time in life, and you aren't there. We want them to know what failure feels like and that is survivable. They go through hard times living away from home; they need the ability to work through the hard stuff. They will know its ok to lean on others, because you let them lean on you when things got sticky. They'll ask for help, because they've been there before and know that it's okay to do so. If we ground them in resiliency now, they will be a strong force for themselves and others in the future.

Communicating

All adults, even 'trained' adults are completely powerless if they do not have the trust of the people, which is where the effort needs to be made, before, during, and after a crisis. It's no use to have training if the kids won't come to you, which is why, when we speak in schools, we're focusing on communication and trust-building. It is a hole that needs to be filled, not just between the faculty and the students but also, between schools, parents, and children so that the good training doesn't go to the wayside because the kids don't consider adults to be safe people to talk to. When the adults model healthy patterns to the kids, they repeat it. If the adults are interacting badly between themselves, the kids are watching, and they give up on the adults and try to handle situations on their own. We want them to trust our motives and responses so that if they need help, they will come to us and not feel shamed. That is how we reduce stigma. Following that healthy pattern, teens see if they have a friend who doesn't feel they have an adult they can go to, the teen who does can get them to the right people for help. We want the kids to know how powerful they are, in the lives of their peers. Healthy relationships are the grounding force of life.

Remember how socially-connected humans are, even from before birth. Babies can hear the voices of their parents and recognize them, once they are born. Our faces respond to their needs with expression and emotions. They learn who they are and how to interact with the world through us. Our kids are intimately connected to us, as their parents. They want us to love them, regardless of the mess, so find that place of connect with them, even if it's going way back to talk about when they were babies.

Families' bonds that have been strained need to be reconnected. The first move is to break them from isolating themselves from you and soften their guarded hearts to let you back in. If your responses have been reactive and unpredictable, it could take time to reassure them that you are a safe person again.

That's why healing your hurts and forgiveness are key before you lean into healing and strengthening your relationship with them. The work you're going to do is not just for the temporary situation that you're going through; it's a time of growth, helping to form your child into an adult that can navigate through life in a healthy way.

The relationships they look for, as they move into the world, will be modeled after what they have at home or what they don't have at home. We want them to be surrounded with good people who are helping them to be a better version of themselves. Don't be frustrated; it's simply a commitment of time and being intentional, in your part of the equation, to nurture the positive. It's not as complicated as some parents are afraid it's going to be.

When we were in youth ministry, I had a mom chase me after church one day, yelling my name. I stopped and turned around to talk to her, and she said, "Melissa, I've been meaning to stop you and talk to you! I have to ask you: what have you done with my daughter?" Of course, I panicked; I had no idea what she was talking about. And, since I have the 'gift of words,' I was worried that I had said something horribly wrong to her child because that 'gift' is also my curse.

She started to tell me a story about a couple of weeks earlier, when she was driving down the main street of our town with her daughter. Her daughter pointed me out and said, "Mom, there's Mrs. Dayton. Pull over—I want to say hi to her!" The mom told me she couldn't pull over. There was traffic everywhere, and there were no parking places. She continued that her daughter began to yell at her, "Mom, Mom! I want to stop and say hello to Mrs. Dayton!" and proceeded to grab the steering wheel to pull the car to the side of the road, at which, the daughter was strongly reprimanded, and they continued home.

The mother looked at me and, again, said, "What have you done with my daughter that she needed to say, "Hello," to you so badly that day? It broke my heart that I couldn't stop the car, and I've been meaning to tell you ever since." Phew, first of all! I can't remember my response, but the conversation followed me home. I went home and told Chip because I really didn't do anything special with her daughter.

We walked through the structure of our meetings with the kids and what stuck out was the first 15 minutes of our time. We would just talk with them, casually, as the kids arrived, by asking them how they were. We would ask them what was going on in their lives or what was happening and made a point of remembering what they loved. We remembered to ask them from week to week how school and their activities were going. That's it.

Sometimes, I think, as adults, when kids have complex issues, we assume, to have an impact on a child in a profound way, we need to have a Ph.D., and we need to be trained or have experience with young people. But, quite honestly, what we learned from that small exchange is that the most profound impact that we have on them comes from our willingness to connect with them at a heart level. It's us, slowing down enough to extend a piece of our hearts so that they feel safe revealing theirs. Teens just want someone to hear them, to appreciate their lives, and to have someone that, without a doubt, will never leave them. They need their cherished adults to be their anchors, as they prepare to move out into the world. Our role changes from caretaker to wisdom person. For us to be effective in that role, they have to trust us on an emotional level. We were able to show that young girl that she was worth our time; she was loved and cherished.

Breaking Barriers

When a child is having a hard time, you think you should step back and give them some space, which they may need, but really, we need to let them know that we aren't going to leave them, no matter how bad things are, no matter how bad their behavior is. How you break down that wall to get back into their hearts may be different for each child, but what I know, for sure, is it will take time.

Open conversation, coming not only from a place of emotional strength but also, a place of compassion, is necessary. Be willing to show them that you aren't perfect. Pretending that you have no weakness, or that you were perfect when you are a teenager is simply going to defeat your child. When you are transparent and open up bravely, you give them a window into who you are, and you give them a gift. When we have done this with our kids, I've actually seen their shoulders soften in relief, and almost always, they open up, in return.

Remind them that all humans are flawed. Opening up to be honest with them is a gift of trust; you are showing them that you trust them to hold information about you that leaves you in a vulnerable place. That is a great and intimate responsibility we hold, as humans, when someone opens up to us, especially when they are bonded to us in family. That is why we need to listen very carefully to them, when they do share, and we need to do so with compassion.

That's why I call being open 'being a gift' or making yourself a gift for others. Allowing those walls to come down is simply being authentic, genuine, and honest, but it takes trust. If you are open first, they will learn, by your example that they can be also. But, remember, what they share from their most wounded or sensitive places, you should handle with care, thoughtfulness, and honor.

Do not use the things they shared to turn on them or tell others, unless it's a spouse. Chip and I are very open with our kids that we will not keep things from the other parent. If our children tell us something, we are a team and are 100% open with one another. We will not lie to them or for them, ever. But, that also reminds them that we will treat them with the same integrity. The trust that your child needs from you should be sacred, with healthy boundaries.

If you're not sure how much to share with them from your teen years, my rule of thumb is: whatever age they are, I try and tell them stories from when I was their age that might be similar to what they're going through or feeling. I would never tell a 12-year-old a story from when I was 17. I'll save those stories because they aren't developmentally prepared for what they might hear.

I know there are adults out there who won't admit to their children that they messed up, drank in high school, or that they ever got in trouble. But, I've also heard their adult children say that they know the truth. The kids want to hear what happened: "How did you resolve the issue?" "Were you in trouble?" "What did you learn?" Hearing your stories and mistakes helps them when they are making decisions. Make sure you are not raving about glory years but instead, teaching from what you learned, even if it's regret.

By giving them a piece of yourself, they relax a bit, and they might be open to sharing with you. It may not happen right away, but eventually, they're going to start to see that you're willing and open to share with them and that you are a safe person to come to. Communication and trust improve when they know you are a safe, non-reactive person. It's why filtering through compassion with honesty, instead of judgment and shame, is so important.

When we have empathy and compassion, unhealthy shame is reduced automatically. Judgement becomes discernment. In our child's eyes, we transform from a judgmental, shaming person that makes them feel that they are bad, to a wisdom person that will help them navigate whatever they're working through. Compassion is the truth, said with love.

Boundaries

It might be a good time to remember that unconditional love does not necessarily mean unconditional approval. Sometimes, our kids are making really bad choices, and we need to be very clear with our boundaries and what we expect from them. We must have predetermined consequences that we are willing to enforce. Discipline and punishment are different. I've found parents afraid to discipline and set up strong limits because they fear being an unjust punisher. Some of what our kids experience in the aftermath is uncomfortable, but the point of consequence is to teach a life lesson. It's again, the difference between a healthy and unhealthy shame. Standing strong with a healthy limit and boundary is a safe place for them to do the hard work.

I have my kids write essays, as part of their consequences, not to give a menial task of nothing, but to give some time to reflect. Chip and I have also had them do things, like alphabetize the CD rack, or weed a garden. Those aren't mindless punishments; those are times for them to diffuse, think, and come to terms with whatever the incident might have been. Simply keeping a teen home by grounding them, without any time for the life lesson, is useless. They stick it out, often in their rooms, on an iPad, watching Netflix. That is a missed opportunity.

When you have done some work on yourself, remember that other people in your life that are stuck in a negative behavior and communication pattern might get frustrated by you changing from reaction to a healthier one. It should not be surprising, if your teenager rages a little bit that you're not reacting and responding to them the way they are expecting, when they push your buttons. Stand confident with kindness. In time, they will see this is the new pattern.

But, this is where consistency comes in; I used to get very angry when the kids were little, and people would say discipline is all about consistency. But, honestly, no two children are the same, and it's almost impossible to have consistent rules and discipline that are the same for each kid. Consistency is needed in emotional reacting and responding; trust with our child is built when they can predict how we're going to respond to a situation.

Which is why those 'what if' conversations at the dinner table are so important. "What would happen if I wrecked the car?" "What would happen if I stole from a store?" "What would happen if I got suspended?" When you have conversations like that, and you've given your child an expectation of your response, they understand what the limits are. They know how you're going to respond to a given situation, based on the proof of how you responded, before and after your conversations.

Are your actions consistent with your words? That is how they tell if you speak truth. That is how teens judge all things.

Beware of Shutting Them down

When you react in a negative way, as they open up and tell you something, you're shutting them down. If you toss out a patronizing comment or cliché, even if you mean it for good, they might clam up. Please be very aware that sarcasm has to be used very carefully with teenagers. I've actually heard lecturers say never but am aware that a dry sense of humor tends to be sarcastic. When your child is hurting, sarcasm cuts like a knife.

When someone is revealing a deep pain or an issue they're working through, and we quickly throw out a cheesy response to fill the space with words, they will clam up. Deeply listen to the words your teens are sharing. Remember that when you're stressed, as an adult, articulating is sometimes difficult. For them, developmentally, they may need quiet space to be able to verbalize the emotions they are feeling, so they need our attention and openness. If you resort to telling them, 'It will all work out,' 'Every cloud has a silver lining,' or 'It's all good,' it could cause them to close themselves off. They shut down, as easily as if you had mocked them. They will smile and nod, but on the inside, they're making note that you really don't understand their pain and won't open up again. It's the difference between sitting with them in their pain and trying to fix it. Sometimes, you can't fix it, and all they want is for you to be with them.

Quite simply, when we open up to one another, we just want someone to hear us. We just want someone to sit with us. When you think of times in your life that you were going through something very difficult and someone was able to just sit with you and be with you without filling the empty space with words, that person, probably, really knew your heart. They knew that there didn't need to be words, or that they didn't have any words to make it better and that you just needed to express whatever you were going through.

When I was in college and pregnant with our oldest son, there was so much pressure on everyone to make that situation work. The adults closest to me were all struggling with their own stresses and worries, and the logistics of how my life was going to work became primary discussion. When I was 5 months pregnant, I went to visit my childhood best friend in Connecticut. She was an only child, and her mom was a second mother to me. It wasn't until I went to see her that I was able to be really honest about how sad I was.

My friend's mom simply sat with me, listened to me, and hugged me. I wasn't upset about having a baby; I knew I could handle all of that. I was terribly and deeply wounded that Chip was gone. He was out of the picture, and I grieved that loss. She was the only one who truly knew that pain; she gave me no advice and didn't try to resolve it. She just listened. Leaving her after that visit, I was stronger. That didn't mean the rest of the pregnancy was a cakewalk, but I knew I was going to be okay.

Being that kind of an adult for a young person is an incredible gift. It's the strength that we found in these wisdom people throughout our lives, if you've been lucky enough to experience it, that have helped us mature. If you make every effort to practice that kind of presence with your child, you give them a gift.

Sometimes, it's your child that repeats the clichés, like 'I'm so dumb,' as a way to stuff what they are feeling and not feel the pain. Acknowledging their pain here and giving them permission to cry or say, 'It sucks,' is really cathartic. They need to know it is okay to cry, be angry, or get mad. But, then, once it's all out, it's time to be stronger, heal, and move forward.

Face Time

Developmentally, infants are constantly searching for that face. A contact in that primal communication, like we talked about before, is essential to who we are, as human beings. Your child can read your face. Whether you want them to or not, they know exactly what you're thinking. They know you as well as you know them. So, when your child comes home, if you're too busy and your face is on your computer or you're reading a newspaper, and they're starting to tell you something, they know you have one hamster in a pot. They know that you aren't giving them your undivided attention.

This is where cell phones are really creating an issue in families. Our children have their face in their phone constantly, and if you don't have limits on cell phone use, or if you don't have a contract with your child, it can get out of control. We need to make sure that our kids understand that the phone is a mode of communication but shouldn't be an extension of their arm 24 hours a day. Eye contact is very important. While texting can get them out of a difficult situation, they really need your face time.

Carving Our Time

Memories are made in good times, but bonds are made in hard times. When the cluster was happening, and Emily was so deeply disturbed by the whole situation, I really had to make time for her. Chip and I backed out of a lot of our extra commitments, and I even backed away from a lot of time that I was usually spending with girlfriends. The days were simple with just time home with my kids. It wasn't only good for my teenagers; it was good for the whole family, especially my last two babies. I really wanted to spend time with them, appreciate, and enjoy them.

Often, I would take Emily with me on walks, but I would also pull her out of school once in a while, we would go out for lunch, or get our nails done. That time I spent with her was a very strong bonding time for us. Sometimes, we talked about what was happening, but other times, we'd talk about nothing. Those times were really important to her and to me. But, I put so much effort into that relationship that when I dropped her off at college and drove off, I said, "What am I going to do, now that I've spent so much time with Emily the last 2 years? I don't think I have any friends left!" To which, Chip responded, "Well, you have me!"

The times she and I spent doing nothing was important. We just couldn't be laser focused on sadness all the time. It's important to take a break from whatever the issue is; they don't want to talk about 'it' all the time. Get creative and create spaces for that time to just be with your child. BUT, it's also important to remember, if you have multiple children, that the other kids can really feel left out, at this point. The last thing you want, while trying to bond with a hard child, is losing another to resentment.

Adults, other than you, are really important and are going to come in handy when you do need to do things with your other kids. Don't feel funny saying yes to the people willing to help give you relief, when the work becomes overwhelming. We saw this over and over with the hurricane. Accepting help can be one of the most uncomfortable things that we do as an adult. But, humbling yourself to accept the help allows people to give you a gift. Simply, say thank you and add them to your joy markers that will become lifelines. When the situation hits a wall and become hard, and some old bad habits start rearing their ugly heads, you'll need to go back to those markers to remember it's temporary and how affirming to know those joy markers are people who love you.

Parenting is a balancing act, and it is a complete sacrifice of your life, as a parent. But, that is what you signed up for. Remind yourself that the joys outweigh all the stress and hard work, like childbirth. You remember the story, not necessarily all the pain, but you definitely remember that moment they placed that baby in your arms. Crisis is the same. You may never be the person you were before, but if you navigate it well, what you'll remember is the good that happened in the process.

Building Them Up—"I Just Want Them to Be Happy"

We can't forget: crisis is temporary. Our primary role as parents, beyond our kids' physical and emotional well-being, is to help them discover their gifts and talents, and ultimately, their vocation of life. A vocation is simply what they were created to do, not just for their own contentment but also, in service to others. True joy and contentment comes from seeing you matter and have purpose in the lives of others. We all want our kids to be happy, but to be honest with you; I'm not as concerned with their happiness as I am with them having a true sense of purpose contentment in life. Contentment is more fulfilling and honest than happy.

I know from experience that a sense of purpose—knowing that you have a profound impact in the lives of others—gives a great, deep joy and contentment that doesn't even compare to happiness. Finding that mission is the hard part. Our kids need us to help them figure out what their purpose is and what their gifts are. We can't tell them, "Be true to yourself," if they have no idea who that is and what they're supposed to do in life. It goes even deeper. I don't mean a job or career. The purpose I mean is the impact they will have, their gifts of character, and temperament that make them unique. Are they compassionate, generous, funny, or a strong leader?

People feel most valued, when they see that they have purpose within a community. Purpose is not simply a task, it is *knowing* and seeing that your work and interactions with others, adds value and is helpful. No one wants to feel that they are being used, unappreciated or are somehow insignificant. Your role as parent is to show your kids see their gifts in action. Name it when you see it, reward it, encourage it and help them discover that purpose.

In this culture, we equate happiness to external or visible gifts. We want our kids to 'have everything' they want, but that's very empty and shallow. We need to watch that easy fix as we're trying repair relationships by just 'buying them' with stuff. If we commit to not handing them every expensive thing we think that they need to have, we have more impact in the formation of their character. It's not just the denying of the item; it's being forced to fill that hole with your time and connection instead.

Waiting is hard, but it's another essential coping skill. Waiting is learned when they have persevered through not having. When we intentionally build them up with purpose and meaning[xii] as a solid foundation in life, not dependent on material goods, those 'needs' dissipate, as well. Please, don't confuse finding purpose with filling up a list of volunteer hours; that's easy to do. Real purpose is seeing that your gifts and talents impact others in a real way and add value to their lives.

When it really comes down to contentment and building resiliency, having a child that grows into an adult who has genuine compassion and empathy for others should be a goal. If they have the courage and bravery to be genuinely kind and impact others before their own wants, then, we've been successful in raising a child that has purpose. Humans are communal. Who we spend our time learning from, as well as impacting, is essential to the people we become.

Mentors are incredibly important in the life of your child, in helping them find that purpose. The summer between sophomore and junior year, when we had the teacher help Andrew, was a time of rebuilding for him and a gift for us, as parents. We watched our son come back into his own and stand strong again. Emily had a teacher in the middle of the cluster that was able to pull out her gift for designing. Another that befriended her became a cheerleader for her. Emily, too, had the experience of adults, other than us, seeing her strength and helping her find her voice. Our son who is in high school now also has a teacher that was able to see deep inside his gifts and challenge him to be the best he could be. He has excelled because of that influence, in ways Chip and I could never have dreamed of. Other strong adults can have profound impacts.

Sensitive Kids

One thing I've noticed in the work we do is that many creative people also suffer from mental illness and feeling deeply. I have to argue against something I see on the internet: the phrase, 'feel too much.' I don't believe anyone feels too much. Creative people feel deeply and the ability to do so is their gift. They are able to express through their words, music, and art emotions that other people can't articulate. Their struggle is their gift, and it's beautiful. We don't want them to lose or stuff that sensitivity by labeling it as 'too much.' We do want to help them notice in themselves when they need relief from what they are feeling and how to find it in a healthy way.

Surrounding themselves with good friends is an additional way to shore up strength.

Friendship

Maybe you have seen YCNBR's video of Emily talking about the cluster and friendship. Her sophomore year, she was fighting to hang out with this group of girls that she wasn't compatible with. They were very sneaky. They were a little on the mean side, but they were a lot of mean on the inside. It was just expected that Emily would lie to Chip and I, go out, drink with them, and go to homes that had no adults. And, when Emily refused to deceive us, they would go three weeks without speaking to her. Emily would walk through those hallways with no one to smile at her or even say hello. It was a very hard time.

Emily, very slowly, started to rebuild her friend group, after I put my foot down and said, 'You can't hang out with these girls anymore.' She went back to someone who was her closest friend in grammar school and very like-minded, from a similar family. She, too, was feeling the same pressures of high school and not wanting to get involved in illegal things. They, very slowly, started to add to their friend circle and rebuilt.

By the time Emily was a senior, she had a great group of friends, both boys and girls: strong kids who had a desire and passion to move forward and grow into better people while still wanting to be 'normal' and have fun. If she had continued to hang out with that original group of girls, she never would have come up with an idea to get involved in the community because they were only focused on themselves. The better friends she ended up with supported her in wanting to see change and encouraged her to make an impact with YCNBR.

You can absolutely encourage those good friendships, even if it's just one. Add fuel to what's good. Find places and ways to provide an 'out' from toxic kids. A general rule of thumb we use in saying, 'no,' is to always be willing to provide an alternative. If you don't provide a safe option, you'll have a resentful kid. So, don't leave a void—provide an alternative. When I told Emily that she was not allowed to hang out with those girls, I, then, had to commit to making myself available for her. My night out with Chip was moved to during the week. The kids ruled the weekend; our house was open. Game nights and fire pits could happen whenever, and if their friends came over, we knew we had to feed those kids lots and lots of food.

Choosing to Have Good Friends Is Modeled: It is a good time to ask yourself who you are spending your time with? If you have friends that are lack integrity, are dishonest, partiers, or cynical about their husbands or wives, are they the best people for you to spend your time with? You will become whom you spend your time with, and your kids are influenced by your peer group, as well. The other adults in our lives have had a tremendous good influence on our kids.

You may need to readjust who is important in your life, if you feel like your message to your child is inconsistent with your choices. Model a healthy example; if your own peer group isn't helping you be the best version of yourself. Introduce yourself to a new community of people and shore up your external structures. Try something new: join a book club, start going to some prevention meetings for parents, and meet people who, maybe, are going through the same things you may be with your kids so that you have stronger external support. Your kids will notice, and your whole family will be better for those new, healthier relationships.

Families need to purposely choose to help our kids discover their gifts and talents that are not just run, jump, be beautiful, or play music. Their true gifts are deeper than that. Compassion and listening or reaching out to someone, when no one else notices them, is a profound gift. As adults, we give them a great gift when we show them how to have that compassion by giving it to them first. The efforts you will make do make a difference, but it's not as complicated as you may fear. Breaking down walls is really tough, when they're angry with you, but if you give a bit of yourself and open up first, they will slowly be curious. They probably have already seen some changes in you over the last couple weeks of working to bring yourself some peace, and trust will grow again: this time, with honesty, authenticity, and deeper roots.

- Make a date with your child. Don't talk about the issue; just enjoy each other.

- Practice listening, with eye contact. It's not easy.

- Try repeating what they have said, and ask if you heard them correctly.

- Respond with wisdom that adds value to the life of your child.

End Thoughts

"Trees that are slow to grow bear the best fruit."—Molière

Chip and I just celebrated 25 years of marriage, and we have been together 30 years. For our anniversary, I put together a video of favorite photos: 30 years of 'making family.' To watch the progression of the birth of each child and how they've grown is moving, but it's also a little exhausting. I can't imagine going back and living it all again. Our life together, raising this family, has been wonderful, but it has also been hard, sad, and challenging at times, although I wouldn't trade the experience or any of my kids for anything.

Parenting has changed who we are, in a good way. We have far more patience and understanding than we did at the beginning. We understand that humans are flawed in a very real way, and we also know that no one goes through the process alone. But, we have also learned that it is essential to stop bad relationship patterns and create healthy ones through perseverance and patience. Healing old wounds is the first step to healing relationships and making sure that does happen. As the saying goes, you cannot pour from an empty cup, but one step further, make sure what you're pouring from the cup isn't toxic.

Developmentally, teens are impulsive, emotional, and swayed by their peers. By giving them a strong bond, founded in integrity and honesty with us, they have a lifeline to come back to when things get hard. The last thing we want them to do is look for 'family' outside our home. But, what we do want them to do is surround themselves with good friends, who will help them be their best, as well as other adults that can help them reach their goals. Those strong relationships will help them get to the right people, if they ever are in a crisis.

Addiction and mental health problems are common, more common than you would think because the stigma surrounding them often silences people. If your family is struggling and feels isolated, the community of people you surround yourself with will help you navigate those situations. We owe it to our children to read and educate ourselves on teen brain development, as well as drug and alcohol trends. But, we also need to watch what kinds of pressure we are putting them under. Are we pushing them for a success that is about our own self-worth?

Unmet expectations, when those expectations are about us, can leave us very disappointed with the life that we have since it doesn't match the one we had hoped for. Sometimes, the emotional distance from a child or the backlash and fighting over consequences to a situation lasts for long durations of time. Those phases of darkness can be hard to shake. Self-care for parents is an important element in teaching resiliency and coping to our kids. They are watching. Finding joy markers throughout the day, though simple, can have profound effects on our outlook in life.

Taking the time to heal after a rough spell in life is a gift you give yourself. The healing and crossroads can be life-changing. Mentors and good friends can help you move forward in a positive way, so make sure you watch whom you spend your time with and how you spend it. Drinking, shopping, and stuffing emotions won't do the work that needs to be done. Instead, positive self-talk, forgiveness, and patience will move you to a different place. Sometimes, that healing takes a long time, especially when the issue with your kid doesn't seem to be going away. But, practicing patience builds a strong resolve and will help you plant your feet in a better place so, as you move forward to reconnect with your child, you are navigating from a place of strength, instead of fear, weakness, and shame.

Having that strength, in comparison, is the difference between reacting versus responding to our children. If we want to be the trusted adult that they can share anything with, then we have to spend time on how well we hear them, when they are trying to open up to us. By filtering their words with compassion, instead of judgement, we respond in a gentle and productive way. If we simply hear to react, we shut them down. There has to be an effort made by us, the adult, to carve out real time with them so they can bring down the walls and start building bridges. All our reading, training, and information are moot, if we do not have their trust.

While we haven't lost a child, we have had a young adult not want to be around us for a very long time, not like us, and seem to reject the family. Gratefully, after a couple years, he has come back into the fold of the family. But, those times take incredible resolve to focus on responding and not reacting from a weak place. The healing for our family, as a result of our consistency and boundaries, has been faster than if we had to do damage control for a lot of arguing and reacting.

The experience of raising children opens windows into ourselves that allows us to expand our thinking, question our ideals, and strips away our own selfish ambitions to focus us on the wellbeing of our family. When we have periods of challenging times, raising our kids, those lessons can be very hard to live day-to-day with. Being overwhelmed is not as uncommon as you would think. Many parents have the experience of being crushed and feeling defeated. The key is how we use the experience. Do we take advantage of the crossroads, and are we willing to strengthen our inner resolve and relationships with our kids?

When we take the time to pause, reflect, and move forward, we are not just growing ourselves—we're strengthening our family ties. Make sure what you are pouring from your cup is full of wisdom. An emotionally-grounded adult has a generous demeanor, in wanting real contentment, not just happiness for their child. Our role is to help them discover their gifts and talent and show them that they have purpose by impacting others. Families are imperfect; they all have times of struggle. Our years as a family living in a community that was suffering were very hard. Our children will be forever shaped by the experience, and so will we.

Our role, as we travel and speak, is our passion because we don't want anyone to live through what we did. We have learned through intense struggles that life can be defeating and sad, but even in the darkest times, small sparks of light can grow into something beautiful. There is no greater reward than having a student come up to us or email us after a talk and share with us that they see themselves differently. Even more profound is when it's an adult who happened to be at the talk.

We want to help heal these hearts; we want to see people breathe easier. We want families to regain their strength and for parents to create a safe place for their children to navigate life. Take the time now, breathe, and trust yourself. You can overcome being crushed. We did, and our family is stronger. In time, yours can be too, and you can share what you have learned with others. Keep moving forward—you will grow, you will change, and you will be okay.

Melissa's Favorite Resources

Personal Growth

Dr. Henry Cloud
Brene Brown
Cheryl Hunter
Maria Schriver
Hal Elrod (Miracle Morning)

Mental Health

Without Tim
Remembering TJ
Jordan Porco Foundation
Erika's Light House
Patrick Kennedy (A Common Struggle)

Substance Prevention

Caron Treatment Center
Behind Beautiful Doors & Pick Awareness
Steered Straight

Extras

Headspace
PrayAsYouGo
Glimmer App (gentle light alarm clock)
The Dirty Goat Soap

*An adult can have the best statistics, education and training available but if they do not have the trust of the young people **they are powerless.***

Melissa and Chip's 5 Tips on Building Trust

1. Eye Contact

2. Predictable responses

3. Healthy expectations

4. Boundaries

5. Active listening

Eyes: Eye contact is a primal and a key piece in human development making it a key component in communication.

- **Refrain from:** Not looking at teens while speaking. There's a hidden message is being sent when someone won't look at us. Disinterest, disapproval, hurt, embarrassment . . . .

- **Focus on:** Undivided attention. Studies have shown that eye contact is healing and builds trust. Let a young person know that they have you are invested in them without judgement. Even if you're upset with something they have done.

Predictable Responses: *Remain calm.* Nothing shuts a teen down and puts up a wall faster than *reacting* *instead of responding.* If you notice your reaction is BIG, then it's time to reflect on why.

Healthy Expectations: Check yourself

- **Refrain from:** Expectations that are about you. Is your self-worth impacted by their actions and choices? Whose self-esteem is being boosted? Are you embarrassed their failures are yours?

- **Focus on:** The teen's personal and emotional growth. Do your expectations add value to their education, experience and path to adulthood?

Boundaries: You are the adult. Healthy boundaries are modeled.

- **Refrain from:** Ridicule, sarcasm, patronizing, name calling

- **Focus on:** Freedom to say yes/no, allowing them to 'feel what they feel', permission to express feelings, support in their personal growth process.

Active Listening: Do you listen to respond or listen to hear?

- **Refrain from:** Stop phrases. Cliché statements that will shut someone down and belittle how they feel. 'It's all good'—maybe it's not? *Talking over.* A great way to shut someone down who needs to be heard is to talk over them and insert your 'advice' before they are done sharing

- **Focus on:** Eye contact, holding space to allow them to cry, vent, and 'hear' themselves. Leading questions—direct the conversation to growth instead of negative thoughts.

Endnotes

i. 'Little': A small child under five. Many parents of large families refer to their bottom half of the family as 'the littles.'

ii. www.cdc.gov/alcohol/fact-sheets/binge-drinking.htm

iii. www.disabilityscoop.com/2009/11/10/autism-moms-stress/6121/

iv. www.pray-as-you-go.org

v. www.headspace.com

vi. www.palmbeachpost.com/news/lifestyles/health/west-palms-hanley-center-hopes-brain-scanner-can-t/nL92g/

vii. www.npr.org/sections/health-shots/2015/01/28/381622350/why-teens-are-impulsive-addiction-prone-and-should-protect-their-brains

viii. www.harvardmagazine.com/2008/09/the-teen-brain.html

ix. Reefer Sanity: Seven Great Myths about Marijuana: Beufort Books, New York 2013

x. www.pickawareness.com

xi. www.behindbeautifuldoors.com

xii. http://sites.gse.harvard.edu/sites/default/files/making-caring-common/files/mcc_report_7.2.14.pdf

Acknowledgements

Thank you to Chip for the patience while this book was being written, and my children who are my heart, challenge, and inspiration to be the best parent I can be.

Special thanks to Dan Windholz for his thoughtful editing, Jen Henderson of Wild Words Formatting for formatting this book, and the parents who have allowed us into their lives to help impact their kids.

About the Cover Art

The cover of Crushed is a pastel painting done by Melissa, who is also an artist, in 2006 after the devastating murder of a boy in their quaint beach community. It was the first loss that rocked local parents and grieved the community. The painting is how many of the adults felt at the time; helpless, wounded and very sad.

Melissa had no idea that beginning in 2008 that sense of being wounded would continue with the loss of 9 students from the high school, 7 to suicide, 2 undetermined. The pain of watching parents lose children is indescribable.

There are times in life when there are no words for the depth of emotion people feel. The painting Good Friday is meant to be a wordless connection to that grief. It speaks volumes to the broken heart, but notice, if she were to look up, she would see the soft glow of light in that darkness . . .

About the Journal Illustrations

The journal illustrations were done in pen and ink by Emily Dayton. Her artwork can be found at One Eye Design on Etsy (www.etsy.com/shop/OneEyeDesigns). Named after her ability to be able to see out of only one eye as the result of multiple surgeries on a corneal dermoid as a baby. Even though she has limited vision, the work she creates is amazingly beautiful. She also played soccer all the way through college, though wasn't great at heading the soccer ball.

Emily graduated Cabrini College in 2015 with a BA in Communications/Marketing and a minor in Fine Art that she acquired during her two years at The University of Dallas. She is the co-founder of You Can NOT Be Replaced and featured in several videos about the organization and what she experienced in high school. In

2013 she was a semifinalist in the Coach Wooden Citizenship award for her work with YCNBR. Emily was one of the cover artists for Lisa Schenke's book, Without Tim, which brought her great joy to be able to contribute to.

Emily is a visual merchandiser for JCrew and lives in New Jersey. You can also follow Emily on her fashion Instagram, The Grace Kelly Effect (www.instagram.com/gk_effect/) or email her questions by going to YCNBR and hitting the contact button.

About the Author

Melissa Dayton is the mother of 8 children and the founder of 'You Can NOT Be Replaced'® which began in 2012 in the wake of a suicide cluster that took 7 high school students from the community.

With her husband Chip and their daughter Emily, they began YCNBR by purchasing 500 passable wristbands to give local kids to use as an excuse to approach another student they may not normally go up to. The wristbands went viral and four years later there are over 50,000 wristbands circulating the USA, Canada, UK and Australia.

Since 2013, Melissa and Chip have spoken to over 30,000 students. The message to the students is to understand their irreplaceable value and the power and influence they have for good in the world. The goal is to improve their relationships so that they have a trusted adult that they are willing to go to when in crisis. Adults can have the best training, but if they don't have the kid's trust they are powerless

Melissa has spent 21 years coordinating youth and family programs. In 2013 she completed a 5 year program with LaSalle University and the Diocese of Trenton with a Master of Arts in Theology and Ministry and pastoral counseling workshops where she studied substance abuse, grief, crisis, healthy communicating and relationships, the teen brain and mental health.

Interested in having Melissa speak at your event or school?
www.chipandmelissadayton.com

Sign up for parenting tips, online workshops, and receive a free
Building Trust Card
www.crushedwhenparentingishard.com

Just have a question or want to send Melissa a message?
youcannotbereplaced@gmail.com

25 Things about Melissa

1. I don't think there are 25 things I can list about me . . . maybe the kids
2. I should be in bed; I have a bad habit of staying up after the kids for quiet, then being tired in the morning.
3. I am VERY blessed
4. I ADORE my husband, even when he makes me mad

Patti Schmidt Photography

5. I have AWESOME kids . . . all of them! They make me laugh and bring me great joy.

Patti Schmidt Photography

6. I would rather be home with my family watching them live and grow than be anywhere else.

7. If I could sleep til 11 every day I would. Of course I wouldn't have to if I would just go to bed already.

8. Life is beautiful, my life is beautiful, I can complain about nothing!

9. I do way too much in a day.

10. I am guilty of getting distracted easily, especially if I don't pray in the am.

11. I thank God for the times that I don't say out loud some of the things I think. I would be in big trouble!

12. I love my faith.

13. I love the women friends God has put in my life.

14. I love the ones who he has put BACK in my life.

15. I wish my brother lived closer.

16. I'm so glad he married his wife, we all like him better now :)

17. I love the beach but would love to live somewhere far away on a huge piece of property.

18. I wish I had a studio to paint in for hours and then just close the door instead of having to clean up.

19. If I'm in the middle of a puzzle, then don't talk to me I'm on a mission.

20. I let my husband put the last pieces in cause I love him but still call him a 'glory stealer'.

21. Every toilet (in my house) I walk by I have to flush . . . because someone forgot to, not because I have OCD.

22. My mantra is 'hang up your coats; put your shoes on the shelf!'

23 I wonder why a boy can write his name with pee in the snow, but can't make it in the toilet

24. I pray all my kids have lives as blessed as us

25. I wish with all my heart I could heal peoples hurts and bring them joy

33414004R00123